PAWSITIVE PERSPECTIVES

Life Lessons from the Shelter Dog
Who Became Queen

By: Carrie Lehtonen

Firefly Media
Evergreen, Colorado

First edition
ISBN (paperback): 979-8-9909152-0-6
ISBN (hardcover): 979-8-9909152-2-0
ISBN (ePub): 979-8-9909152-1-3

Library of Congress Control Number: 2024913055

Ella's Dedication:

I dedicate this book to my human Mom. She accepted me for who I was and has memorialized me by publishing my story.

Carrie's Dedication:

This book is for Ella. She was my loyal sidekick and fellow adventurer for over 15 years, and more importantly, she helped me to become the person I am today.

Table of Contents

Introduction 7

You Deserve Love and Attention 14

You're Perfect Exactly as You Are 17

Have Fun and Appreciate the Little Things 20

If You Want Something, Keep At It Until You Get It
But Don't Get Too Attached 23

Love Unconditionally 26

Eat Regularly, but Be Careful Not to Overindulge 29

Learn and Apply Survival Skills: You Never Know
When You Might Need Them 34

Respect Your Elders. And Cats (They Have Claws) 38

Your Person is Out There, So Don't Settle for Less 42

Maintain Healthy Boundaries 46

Get Plenty of Sleep and Stretch When You Rise 49

Shake It Off.. 52

Hydrate.. 55

Live in the Present Moment. And Be Curious About
the World Around You. 58

Eat Fruits and Vegetables 62

A Dog Might Be Man's Best Friend, but a Kid Is
a Dog's Best Friend.. 65

Take Your Job Seriously, but Make Time for Fun 68

Care More, Do Better 72

Take the Road Less Traveled 75

Trust Your Instincts... 78

Protect Those You Love and Be Cautious of Those
Who Are Out to Get You.. 89

Life is an Adventure ... Climb Aboard! 92

Be Kind, but Don't Be a Pushover....................................95

Walking is Good for Your Health and Happiness
(Body, Mind, and Spirit) 98

Live Your Passion: Never Stop Doing What
You Love 102

Set Your Sights on the Goal, but Take Time to Enjoy the
Journey 106

Celebrate Your Accomplishments 110

Be Determined, and Don't Let a Setback Stop You 113

Be Yourself Without Apology ... but Be Adaptable....116

You're Never Too Old to Learn New Tricks................119

Maintain a Healthy Respect for Water 122

Life is Short, So Don't Put Off What You
Want To Do 126

Be In Awe of the World around You..............................129

Don't Simply Express Your Joy; Unleash It
Wholeheartedly! 132

Don't Stop Learning 135

Never Stop Exploring..138

It's Okay to Accept Help When You Need It,
but Don't Be Helpless 140

Find Your Voice, and Communicate Openly...............144

Do. Dream. Explore. It's Better To Do It First and
Ask For Forgiveness Later. 148

Dogs Know Best, and Humans Need Us.......................151

Epilogue 155

Notes 162

Resources 164

Acknowledgments 166

About the Author...172

Introduction

This is a love story and a manual for how to live life, all told from the perspective of a special dog who defined a decade-and-a-half of my life. Ella was born a stray, but that didn't stop her from climbing her way to the position of Queen of the Lehtonen household. But I'm getting ahead of myself.

Our story began in June 2006 at the Denver Dumb Friends League shelter in Denver, Colorado. Ella had been turned into the shelter by a family who had found her as a puppy in a field beside a busy street. They stated that she was "too much" for their older dog, but good with chickens (go figure), so they brought her to the shelter so she could find a more appropriate home.

It was a twist of fate that led me to meet Ella that day. I had left work in the middle of the day to meet an adorable Australian Shepherd puppy at the shelter who had previously been on hold for someone else but was now available. I had had my eyes on that pup for a couple of weeks, but per the rules of the shelter, no one can "reserve" a dog over the phone – you must do it in person.

When I saw that the puppy was suddenly available for adoption again, I asked my manager if I could leave to get to the shelter right away. He was an animal lover too. "Yes, of course," he said. I jumped in my car and headed off.

The shelter was an hour away and I called when I was about halfway there, only to be told that the puppy had been adopted. I was devastated! I decided to stop at the shelter's primary location to meet some other dogs since by that time I was desperate for a dog. I had been living in my new house for three months at that point…it had a big fenced-in backyard and no dog to play in it, although my cat Anabelle liked the yard well enough.

I grew up with dogs. From the moment I was born my family always had at least two dogs in the house, a cat (or two), and sometimes guinea pigs, fish, or rabbits. When I moved from New Hampshire to Colorado in January of 2005, I brought my cat with me but was eager to add a dog to our family, although it didn't make sense to do that until I moved out of my apartment and into a house. This happened in March of 2006, at which point I started watching the shelter's list of adoptable dogs.

When I met Ella that fateful day in June, her name was Lassie. She was a five-month-old German shorthaired pointer mix, who had kennel cough at the time, so I had to meet her in a special area. I was hoping for a running buddy, so when I started jogging around the outdoor kennel area and she clung to my side, I knew she was the one. Ella was quiet, but curious, with brown, almond-shaped eyes that could melt your heart in an instant. She had dark brown fur with a white-speckled chest and socks, and floppy ears that changed position depending on her mood. I knew she would make a good sidekick for the many adventures I had planned. That was that, I was hooked. I signed the forms, and we were on our way to start fifteen years and three months of adventurous life together. This was time that would shape the rest of my life.

Ella found her voice shortly after she recovered from kennel cough and settled into her new home with me and Anabelle. Ella had more personality than any dog I had met before her. She was full of surprises and kept me on my toes. Even as a puppy, she had an air of wisdom. I could tell that she was always watching, listening, and thinking.

We went hiking, camping, running, paddle boarding, and traveling around the country. Boyfriends came and went, but Ella was always there to lick my tears when relationships went south. She helped keep my spirits up after two knee surgeries, a heart attack at a young age, job changes, and ultimately starting my own business. She was there through a decade and a half of my evolution. My years with Ella were transformative.

After surviving a heart attack at 31 years old I went into a bit of a tailspin. Being told that you wouldn't have survived the night if you hadn't come to the hospital are impactful words for someone in the prime of life. I wasn't sure what else to do but I knew I didn't want to spend the rest of my life working in the corporate world. Ella helped me see that while it's important to take your work seriously, you also need to enjoy life and follow your passion. I followed my heart and pursued certifications in health coaching and teaching yoga. Now, I own and operate my own wellness business, Firefly Community LLC, to help others ignite their inner lights so that they can thrive and shine.

Firefly provides services and events for individuals and groups. We lead and coordinate yoga and wellness retreats internationally and domestically. We provide a supportive community and resources, such as a holistic wellness coaching program and group and private yoga classes so our clients can thrive. Firefly serves the corporate community by offering onsite and virtual yoga classes, and wellness, mindfulness, and stress management workshops.

Ella assumed the role of big sister when I added two kittens and another puppy to our family when she was about eight years old. She happily welcomed the third boyfriend with the name of John, who later became my husband. (Dogs do have a sense about people, and she was right about this John being a keeper). With all the changes, Ella made it clear that she was the boss. She had many nicknames over the years, but most often, we lovingly referred to her as the Queen.

In 2018, when Ella was twelve years old, we noticed while on the way down from a tough hike in Bozeman, Montana that her back legs were a bit shaky and crossing at times. She soldiered on and kept hiking with us. About a year after that hike in Montana, Ella started dragging the toes on her back feet. We consulted a vet, who told us it could be degenerative myelopathy (DM), which develops over time. It's a disease in which the nerve's ability to transmit signals gradually decreases, leading to weakness and eventually paralysis starting in the back legs. DM is similar to some forms of ALS (Lou Gehrig's Disease) in humans. It's not painful, since they lose feeling in the impacted areas, and dogs can lead perfectly good lives for a period of time, although the amount of time can vary significantly from dog to dog. Eventually, the paralysis moves forward and can start impacting the organs. Our vet emphasized that you never want to wait until it's gone that far.

No test can definitively determine that a dog has DM until after they die, but they can test to see if the dog has one or two genetic variants that indicate the likelihood of ending up with DM. We never did the test, but the symptoms were all indicative that Ella had it. We bought all kinds of products to help her back feet: booties, socks, stickers for her pads to give her more traction, and "toe-ups." She started acupuncture in December of 2019, and physical therapy not long after that. She began using a Walkin' Wheels® wheelchair in early 2021 when she could no longer use her back right leg. We got a sling to help her around the house. It took all of us a while to adjust, but we made it work, and Ella was still happy as a clam.

We took Ella on her last road trip in April 2021 to the Grand Canyon. She loved it, as I knew she would. In August 2021, two days before we were supposed to go camping, Ella suddenly appeared to be in pain. I stayed up all night with her and kept trying to help her shift her position to make her more comfortable. I propped her up on blankets and two dog beds. By morning, I had talked to the emergency vet and the service that comes to your house to euthanize dogs. She was scheduled to be assisted to the other side later that morning. We gave her doggie ice cream, I read her a letter I wrote for her, and we were all by her side when she closed her eyes for the last time. The vet who came to help her transition thought that perhaps Ella had a cyst that had burst since it was too sudden to have been related to the DM. Ella decided her time had come to say goodbye. It was tearful and gut-wrenching.

Ella taught me a lot about being present, living life to the fullest, and loving unconditionally, among other things. Through this book, I want to share these lessons with you ... from Ella's perspective, because I'm certain she wouldn't have it any other way. Throughout the chapters, Ella refers to me as "Mom."

I hope you find Ella's thoughts on life to be as useful as I did and are entertained by her antics. Perhaps Ella's life story can make the world a more joyful place and remind us of the important role that our pets play in our lives. Each of the following chapters shares one lesson. While it may be easier to follow the story by reading the chapters in order, feel free to jump around as you wish. May Ella's wisdom touch your heart and inspire you to be true to yourself and follow your dreams.

Sincerely,

Carrie Lehtonen

Evergreen, Colorado

https://fireflycommunity.com

info@fireflycommunity.com

You Deserve Love and Attention

"You yourself, as much as anybody in the entire universe, deserve your love and affection."
—Gautama Buddha,
founder of Buddhism

When I was staying at the shelter in Denver, I knew that the right person would come along who would love me and treat me like the queen I am. I never expected anything less. Sometimes people forget their worth. They might let people into their lives who don't love and respect them. They end up in relationships where they aren't treated well and, unfortunately, they eventually believe that they don't deserve anything more. But that's not true!

We all deserve to be loved. You can tell that dogs wholeheartedly believe this because we love unconditionally. Everyone makes mistakes or does things we're not proud of, but that doesn't mean we shouldn't receive love and attention. In fact, in many cases, those are the times that we need love the most. When someone tells you that they love you, no matter what, it helps you to love yourself. It's only when you love yourself, that you can truly love another.

I knew I had my faults, but I was also fully aware that those didn't define me or my worthiness for love. Just by being myself, I was worthy. I was already complete exactly as I was. Sure, I always wanted to learn more, and do better, but that didn't mean I wasn't perfect as is. We're all unique, and we come from different backgrounds and circumstances. Our differences make us special. Mom saw that I wasn't your typical dog, and she loved me as I was. She gave me affection when I needed it, and sometimes when I didn't even want it. I pretended to be annoyed, but secretly I appreciated that she showered me with love all the time.

Mom gave me a lot of hugs and told me that I was the best hugger. I was apparently the perfect height for her to bend down and put one arm around my back between my front legs and around my chest, with the other arm around my neck. In that position, she would plant a kiss on my snout. Mom loved to put her face against mine to look me right in the eyes and tell me what a good dog I was and how much she loved me. She also knew how much I liked it when she'd put a knuckle just inside my ear (not too far) and give it a little scratch. I would groan to show how much I appreciated the show of affection.

There will always be people who tell you that you need to do or be something else for them to love you. If that happens, move on. They're not in a place where they can give you what you deserve. Maybe they weren't treated well in the past and have some things to work through, but it's not your job to fix that. If they don't treat you right, find someone who will. Being able to give love starts with loving yourself. The sooner you believe you don't have to earn love the better off you'll be.

You're Perfect Exactly as You Are

You don't need to change anything to be deserving of love, because you're perfect exactly as you are. Sure, we all have experiences that leave us a bit tattered and torn, but we are all unique, beautiful beings.

My bio at the shelter said I had been found in a field in Broomfield (a suburb of Denver). A family had taken me in for a bit, but their older dog wasn't a fan of my puppy energy, so they turned me in to the shelter. I didn't fit in with what they were looking for, but it didn't mean I wasn't perfect exactly as I was.

Humans go through life thinking that someday they'll get to this magical place where everything will be perfect. But the truth is you were already perfect from the day you were born. Your body contains your spirit, your innocent soul. People spend a lot of time worrying about their bodies – whether it's thin enough, muscular enough, or if they're tall enough. None of that matters at all. It's what's inside your heart that matters, and your heart is pure. You are love. Your experiences might make you forget your true nature from time to time, but that's all part of being human. What matters is that you do your best and are kind to others.

In my lifetime, I started hearing about social media and how it made people feel "less than" because they spent a bunch of time looking at polished posts – the version of themselves they wanted others to see. That's not reality. Life can be messy, and that's the beauty of it. You weren't sent here to be perfect. You were sent to a human body to screw up and learn from your mistakes, to lose your way, but to get back on track. There's no such thing as perfect. Perfection is an illusion—just like those social media feeds, and airbrushed photos all over the internet.

Your idiosyncrasies are what make you, you. There's no one else like you in the world, so do the world a favor and be yourself. Because if you're not, who else is going to do it? No one else can do better at playing you than you can. The world needs the special gifts you were sent here to share. Stop worrying about what other people think. I bet your dog loves you, and that should tell you something because dogs know a thing or two about love.

Mom was always fretting about her pants getting tight. I'm here to tell you, forget about trying to fit into the same size you did in college because it doesn't matter. All that's important is that you are happy. Worrying about small things isn't going to improve your mood. I didn't worry about being perfect. I lived my life the way I wanted to and expressed who I was. It didn't matter what the other dogs were doing, I was my own dog.

The next time you take a look in the mirror, tell yourself that you're beautiful, because, my dear, you are! If you catch yourself thinking something negative about yourself, pause and replace that statement with a positive. The more you practice being nice to yourself the easier it will be. Most of the things you say to yourself, you'd never say to a friend. Treat yourself the way you would treat a friend. And remember, you're perfect exactly as you are!

Have Fun and Appreciate the Little Things

"Enjoy the little things, for one day you may look back and realize they were the big things."
—Robert Brault

I really loved Christmas. Mom would always wrap at least a few things for me so I could experience the joy of opening gifts, even if it was just a box of treats I already knew about. The process of ripping the paper and using my teeth to tear away anything that stood between me and my gift made me happy.

Even when it wasn't Christmas, when packages arrived at the house, delivered by a man in a big brown truck, I always thought it was for me. Mom got such a kick out of watching how joyfully I would rip open boxes, that she would often take out whatever item had arrived for her, put a couple of treats in the box, and then let me at it. She was always sure to make it possible for me to open the box on my own without a ton of damage because she didn't want to pick up a million pieces of cardboard off the floor after I was done. It made her laugh to watch me use my skills to get at whatever was inside the package.

This backfired on Mom a couple of times because I would get so excited that I would open boxes that weren't intended for me. Grandma once sent Mom a wireless charger for Mom's new Bluetooth headphones, and I got to the box under the Christmas tree. In my efforts to get it open, my tooth went through the box into the charger and cracked it. Luckily it still worked.

Sometimes the packages that arrived were for me. I loved when my uncle would send me a new collar he had made special just for me. He owns a business, CritterGear, making dog and cat collars, leashes, and toys. I had quite the wardrobe, with a different collar for most holidays. I liked it when Mom would slip a brand new one over my head and tell me how pretty I looked.

Opening boxes and getting new collars were small things, but I appreciated them. It was kind of Mom to recognize how much joy it brought me, and to give me lots of opportunities to open gifts over our years together. And it was sweet of my uncle to make all of my collars.

Humans often think it's the big things that will make them happy (like a fancy house, a high-paying job, or a new car). But the reality is that happiness is made up of the small things—the moments that you'll look back on someday that will still bring a smile to your face. What is your equivalent of my opening boxes? What brings you joy, and is fun for you? Be sure to make time in your life for whatever it is.

If You Want Something, Keep At It Until You Get It But Don't Get Too Attached

"Just as phenomena arise let them be and do not cling."
—Shabkar Tsokdruk Rangdrol,
Tibetan Buddhist

There's no doubt that once I set my mind to something, I would achieve my goal. When I was a puppy, I would work on tearing open my toys until I managed to get the squeaker out. I loved to lay there and just squeeze, squeeze, squeeze, making lots of noise with those little plastic parts inside the toy. Some toys were harder than others to rip apart, but I would find the weak spot and work on it until I got it open. I was determined to get that squeaker out, but the point of sharing this story is to tell you to not get too attached. Once I had squeaked to my heart's content, I would move on to the next thing.

There were many things I was interested in doing and getting, and I usually succeeded. If there was a trash bin hidden in a cabinet under the kitchen sink, I would open the cabinet door, pull the bin out, and proceed to pull every last bit of trash out of the bag to look for anything good. If there was food in a drawer at my level, I would figure out a way to open that drawer and eat whatever was inside. If there was a zipped bag in the car with treats in it, I would open the zipper to get inside. My ability to do all of those things might surprise some people, but I knew what I wanted and wouldn't let anything stand in my way. It might take multiple attempts, but I eventually honed my skills in all of these tasks and they became easier each time I had the opportunity to do them.

I didn't get too hung up on anything. Some dogs are crazy about chasing the ball. They'll bring it back to their human over and over until one of them is too exhausted to continue. I preferred variety. I did chase a ball once or twice, but then I wanted to go check out a new smell or visit with a person who came by. Sure, I was attached to Mom, but I gave her space—I wasn't right by her side all of the time. If I knew she was safe, like inside the house working at her desk, I would go do something else. If we were at the dog park, I would trot off to check out all of the smells along the fence line.

It's important to have goals, but things change constantly. You can't get too attached to one outcome. Things might not turn out the way you planned but chances are you'll end up with exactly the situation you needed. The trick is to find the gift in what *is* and stop worrying so much about what was or what will be. If you live in the present moment, you'll be better able to go with the flow of life and deal with whatever comes your way.

Love Unconditionally

"If you can love me for what I am, we shall be the happier."
—Ralph Waldo Emerson

I don't think anyone knows how to love quite like a dog does. We love our humans unconditionally, even when they hurt us, which unfortunately happens more than it should. I'm lucky my mom loved me unconditionally, too, even when I drove her crazy.

When Mom first adopted me, she had to leave our house to go to work during the weekdays. I was lonely without her, but at least I had a doggie door and could go outside in the backyard and keep an eye on the neighborhood. Even though Mom always made sure we got out for a walk or jog before or after work, I was thrilled beyond belief when Mom finally left that job and started working at home every day.

Whenever Mom returned home, even if she had just gone to the grocery store, I would greet her with enthusiasm—lots of tail-wagging and barking, and even an occasional kiss. I didn't care if it was three minutes or three days, I wanted her to know how happy I was to see her. Mom did still travel even after she started working at home—probably less than she wanted, but more than I wanted. When she came back from a trip, I would wrap my paws around her arm to hold her there. I would shake and whine to let her know just how much I had missed her.

Even though I wasn't what one might consider a cuddly dog, I loved to sit close by and have Mom pet me. If she would stop before I was satisfied that I had sufficiently calmed her nervous system by letting her pet my head and touch my soft ears, I would nuzzle her hand with my nose to put her hand back onto my head. Mom absolutely loved my ears and enjoyed how silky and soft they were.

I took care of Mom and tried to let her know when I thought she was spending time with someone who didn't treat her right. She had one boyfriend in particular whom I did not approve of. When we arrived at his place for a visit, I would jump out of the car and run away from his house. His sister lived down the block, and she was a good person so I would head there instead. Mom finally listened to me, and one night after a big fight, during which he scared me with his shouting, we left and never went back.

Dogs have a sense about people and know the good ones from the not-so-good ones. When Mom started dating a third boyfriend named John, I liked him right away. All my signals to Mom about him were positive, and lucky for both of us, she listened to me again. He soon was part of our family, and eventually became my dad. He loves Mom just as much as I do and takes good care of her.

I wish all humans would learn to love as much as dogs do, but I understand sometimes their life circumstances can cause them pain, making it hard to love. But love is what we are all born with; it's just a matter of unlearning the fear the world can cause and opening your heart again. Having a dog companion in your life can help in that regard. We can remind you what it means to love, and how good it feels to not only receive love but to give it as well. As humorist Josh Billings once said, "A dog is the only thing on earth that loves you more than he loves himself."

Eat Regularly, but Be Careful Not to Overindulge

My insatiable hunger and quest for food at all costs started early in my life when I was fending for myself on the streets before I was picked up and turned into the shelter. I didn't have to survive on my own for long, but any amount of time not knowing where your next meal is going to come from has a lasting impact on a dog. I was just a puppy, after all.

Mom says I was the most food-motivated dog she had ever met. The dogs she lived with growing up always had food in their bowls and would just eat whenever they were hungry. Not me. If there was food in my bowl, I ate all of it—it didn't matter how much food. I would finish whatever was in the bowl in about thirty seconds flat.

I slept in my bed at night, but in the morning, I would jump up onto Mom's bed to wake her up so she could give me breakfast. She thought it would be better for me to go outside and relieve myself first, but I taught her there was no way I was doing anything until I'd eaten. I got very excited about my meal. Who cares if it's the same thing every day—it's food! As a young dog, I would jump and spin until the food hit my bowl, and then devour it as fast as possible. I had a sitter once who used to make me sit down before she would put the food in my bowl. That drove me crazy, but she was tough and didn't let me get away with my usual antics.

At dinner time, if Mom wasn't home from work yet, I would go through my doggie door into the backyard and bark to let all of the neighbors know I was hungry and not sure if Mom would ever get home. But inevitably she would show up, sometimes later than usual, and I'd finally get fed.

My motivation for food helped me get my certificate in puppy training school. I was the fastest to complete tasks because I couldn't wait to get my treat! For most of my life, I would run through my whole series of known tricks to get my treat. It didn't matter which trick Mom was asking me to do, I just did all of them so I could get it over with and get my reward.

When we hosted holidays or cookouts at our house, Mom had to make sure I wasn't left unattended near any food, or I would gobble it up. If Mom had to leave the room when she was in the middle of cooking or had left something on the counter out of my reach, I would whine because I was worried she had forgotten about it. I didn't want any food to go to waste—that would be a tragedy! This habit of mine came in handy a few times when Mom had forgotten that she left something out.

I was obsessed with food, which meant I was also a persistent beggar. I always watched Mom eat, giving her my best sad eyes to let her know I was starving. If she didn't pay attention, I would start whining. I stayed close by when anyone was in the kitchen, waiting for anything to hit the floor or for Mom to hand me some scraps. Mom called me her "gluten girl" because I had a special affinity for pizza, in particular, and also bread and pasta. I particularly liked crunching away on dry, uncooked pasta.

I looked for (and found) food everywhere. Mom kept my food in a large plastic bin with a latching top. She usually kept it in the laundry closet where I couldn't get to it since I couldn't open those doors. There were a couple of times when the doors weren't shut completely, and I managed to chew that cover enough to pop it open and feast to my heart's content. I ate so much I had to lie down, and when Mom felt my belly, she exclaimed that it was hard as a rock. Even though I felt kind of sick, I still begged for dinner that night. Mom still has that bin with my teeth marks in the top.

One of the times I got into my food bin, I felt so yucky I had to go find my favorite squeaky toy (Lamby). I went into the bedroom and lay on my bed with Lamby. Mom wasn't sure what was up with me until she found the open food container and realized I had overeaten again. Lamby was providing me with comfort.

Mom learned early on not to leave me in the car with any food. On the way to a camping trip, Mom had to grab something else from the store quickly, so she left me in the car with everything that had already been packed for the trip. While she was gone (only a couple of minutes), I ripped open a bag of hamburger buns and ate all eight of them. Even I was impressed with how quickly I managed to get all of those down the hatch. After that day, Mom never left me in the car with any food. She would even bring bags of food in with her if she had to run in somewhere when we were on a road trip. She didn't trust me not to rummage through the bags and help myself.

I could open drawers, so Mom didn't keep any food in the lower drawers in our house. One day she left me unattended at a boyfriend's house, and I figured out that one of the kitchen drawers had a bunch of protein bars inside. I ate four or five of those high-calorie bars, coated in chocolate, which turned out to be a bad idea. Later that night, I threw up in the bedroom closet, which no one was happy about.

Around the holidays one year, Mom left a bowl of Lindt truffles on the entertainment center in the living room and went to work. She thought it was out of my reach since the entertainment center was fairly tall, and she had pushed the bowl back. I managed to find a way to get to that bowl and ate probably eight chocolate truffles. Mom said I must have an iron stomach because I never got sick after that escapade. Those truffles were delicious!

My desire for food got me into plenty of trouble, but the worst was when Mom's boyfriend (the one who later became my Dad) left me alone in the car with his friend's backpack. His friend didn't know about my skills. It didn't take me long to unzip that backpack and eat his whole bag of chocolate-covered raisins. I didn't know I wasn't supposed to eat raisins and, frankly, I didn't care. I ended up in the pet hospital for a few days after that debacle. John hung out with me in the hospital on New Year's Eve because he was so worried about me. That's how I knew he cared and was a keeper.

As you can see from my experiences, sometimes overindulging in foods, especially certain things, turns out to be a bad idea. You need to make sure you're getting enough to eat to give you the energy to do all of the fun things you want to do but be careful not to overdo it, or you might get sick.

Learn and Apply Survival Skills: You Never Know When You Might Need Them

I was a survivalist, which is why I made it almost to age sixteen, despite having degenerative myelopathy towards the end. I had specific skills that I applied in various dangerous situations.

When I was a young pup, I wasn't afraid of thunderstorms, but one day I was out on a run with Mom, and we got stuck in a hailstorm at the absolute furthest point from the house with nowhere to take cover. We had to run as fast as our legs could carry us, while getting pelted by hail, to get home.

After that day, any time there was the slightest rumble of thunder, I would take cover wherever I could. Most often I hid in the bathtub. Hours later, I would make my way back out when the danger had passed. If the bathroom wasn't available (i.e., if a storm happened at night and we were in the bedroom), I would squeeze myself under the bed. Mom made the mistake of getting a new bed that was lower to the floor, so I had to lay next to the bed and just have my paws underneath—it wasn't great, but it was better than nothing!

The worst scenario was if I happened to be in the backyard when a storm rolled in suddenly. In that case, I crawled under a wooden platform next to the fence. It was pretty tight under there; I had to dig down into the dirt a bit to get myself fully covered. Mom would try coaxing me back out, but it was even more of a struggle to get out.

One particularly snowy and windy winter day, we were out snowshoeing. I felt it was too dangerous to keep moving, so I stopped and started digging a hole in the snow. I had it deep enough for me to curl up in when Mom and her friend got me to agree to keep moving. We turned around to take a different trail that didn't have such a headwind. Mom asked when I had taken a winter survival class, but it was just my keen instincts that caused me to dig that snow shelter.

I was never a fan of camping. The first time I ever slept in a tent was when Mom decided it would be fun to go camping with a group of friends to celebrate her thirtieth birthday. A couple of Mom's friends brought stuff to make s'mores over the fire, which was fine by me since I got some graham crackers out of the deal. Unfortunately, they left the bin with the s'mores supplies outside that night. After we'd all gone to bed, a fox (or some kind of wild animal) came along and got into the container, then came sniffing around our tent. I was so scared that neither I nor Mom slept a wink that night.

We went camping about once a year. Every time Mom would pull out my air mattress dog bed and set it by the fire for me because I did not like to lie down in the dirt. My bed was okay, but anytime a fellow camper would get up to use the bathroom, I would pop up and steal their chair. A chair is definitely better than lying on the ground!

When it would come time to go to sleep, I would walk towards the car to try to remind Mom that we didn't need to sleep outside with only a thin piece of nylon between us and the wild animals and any potential storms. We owned a house, for goodness' sake, or we could always stay at a hotel. I loved fancy hotels. My favorite hotel was Elevation in Crested Butte, Colorado, a four-star hotel. The first time we stayed there, there was a bellhop who catered to my every need. "Oh, you need some treats? Let me get some for you." Or "You forgot Ella's bed in the car, I'll go get it and bring it to you." Adam was great!

Anyway, back to survival. I was always up for an adventure, but I didn't have a lot of faith in my sometimes-irresponsible mom to keep us safe, so I did my part to ensure our survival. On windy roads, I would get on the floor of the car between the back seats and front seats to be in the area of the car least impacted by the curves.

In the summer months, if we didn't start our hike early enough, and it had warmed up too much, I would trot from shady spot to shady spot along the way. I would move as fast as possible through the sunny areas to get to the shade where I could take a break. I'm sure you can understand—my dark fur soaked up the heat from the sun, and it's not like I could take my fur coat off. I was always sure to drink enough water too, but I'll cover that in more detail later.

Be sure to always check the conditions before you head out on an adventure, and bring what you need to stay safe. Be prepared for sudden weather changes, especially when in the tall peaks of Colorado, when a storm can roll in at any time. Get to know your surroundings and stay alert at all times. If you apply these skills, you'll enjoy a long, healthy life.

Respect Your Elders. And Cats (They Have Claws)

"Dogs may chase cats, but even the most rambunctious pup recognizes the quiet power of a feline stare. Maybe it's not respect, but a healthy dose of caution and curiosity."

—Unknown

When Mom first adopted me, she already had a cat who ruled the household: Anabelle. Mom told me Anabelle had been with her since before she was born. Mom had taken in a stray cat who turned out to be pregnant. Jasmine gave birth to four fluffy, black and white kittens underneath the futon in Mom's apartment in New Hampshire. Anabelle was the runt of the litter. When she was little, she looked like she had stuck her paw in an electrical socket, because her fur stood on end. She was the most adventurous of the kittens—slipping her way across the linoleum into the kitchen to explore while her brothers and sister remained within the safety of the carpeted living room. She used to climb Mom's pant leg to get to her shoulder while she was washing dishes or watching TV.

Mom always appreciated a fiery spirit, so she decided to keep Anabelle and found homes for the other kittens and Jasmine. They went everywhere together, and Anabelle moved across the country with Mom. They spent four days (thirty-two hours in the car) to get to Colorado. At first, they lived in an apartment, but when they moved into a house, that's when I came into the picture.

Anabelle quickly established herself as my elder. I was more than willing to respect her, and we lived together in harmony. But that didn't mean I had to like all cats. Anytime a neighborhood cat would pass by I would alert everyone.

Mom once dated a guy with two cats, one of whom seemed smitten with me. When we'd go for a walk, this cat would wait outside for us to return. When we got back, he'd run to greet me, but like any self-respecting dog, I would walk right past him with no acknowledgment. I knew I had to live with him, but I didn't have to be overly friendly.

Poor Anabelle was diagnosed with kidney disease at age seven. Despite Mom's efforts of providing her at-home fluid treatments and special food, we had to say goodbye to Anabelle about a year later when her health took a sharp turn for the worse and the doctor told us she wouldn't recover. After that, it took Mom many years before she could even consider adopting another cat.

We didn't add another cat to the family—two in fact—until 2014! Mom was talking to her manager on the phone and found out he was fostering kittens who needed homes. He sent her a picture and a particular little tortoise-shell-colored fluff ball caught her eye. She went to meet her and decided to adopt both her and her sister. When mom went back about a week later the sister was no longer available. She still thought it would be good to adopt two cats so they could play together, so the foster family talked her into taking the runt of the litter along with the tortie. The runt had tiger stripes, a white half-mask, and a white belly and legs. Each of the kittens weighed two pounds.

When Mom brought the kittens home that night, I sat on the floor with them in the guest bedroom until Kali (the tortie) hissed at me. I knew cats have claws, so I hid under the bed for the next hour to be safe. At some point, that little kitten decided I was her best friend. She followed me around, slept in my bed with me, and got as close as I would allow. I was not pleased. I didn't need a cat as a friend. But later I appreciated her ability to get views from a higher vantage point in the backyard since as a cat she could climb trees. Mateo (the tiger) also liked being around me, but he found his true love ten months later when a dog who became our new sister, Mala, came into our lives.

Even though they were a different species, each of the cats was a member of our family, so I respected them. I didn't always like having to hang out with them, but I did my duty as their sister and protected them. It turns out cats aren't so bad as long as you don't give them a reason to use their claws against you. We're all more alike than we are different, and it's important to respect others.

Your Person is Out There, So Don't Settle for Less

The people who found me in that field when I was a puppy said I had a bit too much energy for their family, but that's okay, it just wasn't the right fit. I knew my person was out there, even while I was staying at the animal shelter. When I first met the woman who was to become my forever mom, I knew she was the person for me. She was young, active, and had a big heart. I could tell right away we were kindred spirits, and I was right—we were both adventurers and liked to do many of the same things.

Mom grew up with dogs and cats (and rabbits, guinea pigs, and fish) in her family. And that's exactly what they were, members of the family. She never looked at me as "just a dog" as some people might. I was her child from the day she brought me home. She found out pretty quickly that I wasn't like other dogs she had loved over the years. I had a unique personality. Of course, I was loyal, but I had a mind of my own. I was smart and she appreciated my independence, given that she was independent, too. As the elf says in *Rudolph the Red-Nosed Reindeer*[1], we decided to "be independent together!" Mom watched that old movie every Christmas. It was the perfect relationship, and we both knew it. I wanted to be sure she always stayed with me, so when she returned from a trip, I would grab onto her arm with both my paws and hold on tight.

As I mentioned, Mom dated several guys during our many years together. Some were better than others, and I got along fine with most of them. I didn't like it one bit when Mom found herself in a relationship with an angry, controlling man who would often yell at her. Mom would mostly stand her ground, but she put up with a lot from him, thinking that he loved her. It wasn't until one night when he yelled at me that she finally left him. She took a lot of crap from him but didn't accept him being a jerk to me—her innocent baby.

I guess she finally realized she didn't deserve to be treated that way, either. We all deserve to be treated with care and respect, and what he was doing to her wasn't okay. We all make mistakes or do things we're sorry about. That doesn't give anyone the right to make us feel bad about ourselves. I knew when I did something I shouldn't. I showed Mom my "I'm sorry" grin when she would get home, knowing she might be mad at first, but that she loved me and would forgive me. She would look into my sad eyes and tell me it was okay. Nothing could take away her love for me.

I was ecstatic when after that disappointing relationship, Mom met a guy who was just as kind-hearted as her. I knew immediately that this John (mom dated three guys named John in a row!), was a keeper. I think in her heart, Mom knew it too, but this John was ten years younger than her, so they were both a little cautious at first. It didn't take them long to realize they were each other's person.

I knew this guy was going to last when about a year after they started dating, they adopted a puppy together. I was with them when they met the little fluff ball who would eventually be named Mala. They weren't looking for a dog, but Mala chose us. Just like my adoption, it seemed meant to be. I tried to convey that I wasn't interested in getting a new sister, but Mom was particularly drawn to Mala when she fell asleep in Mom's hands. They adopted Mala, and she turned out to be a good sister and a great addition to our growing family.

This third (and last) John asked Mom to marry him at the end of 2016, and about six months later, they tied the knot with Mala and me as the ring bearers. The wedding was beautiful, and Mala and I got to be there (for the ceremony at least), we didn't get to attend the reception, much to my dismay. My smile was as wide as ever that day watching them say their vows to each other. I'm so glad Mom never settled for any of those other guys so she could meet the right one for her. I was proud that she figured out what she deserved and waited until she found it before deciding to give me a human dad. Mom had found her person at last. I always knew she would.

Maintain Healthy Boundaries

"Setting boundaries is an act of self-love. It is your way of saying, 'I matter,' and I deserve to be treated with respect."
—Unknown

I loved my family and enjoyed being fawned over and petted but on my terms. When I wanted attention, I would go over to Mom and nudge her hand in a request for her to pet me. If she stopped before I wanted her to, I would nudge her again, and keep at it until I was satisfied. I did the same thing with members of our extended family and friends. Whenever possible when we were out walking or hiking, I would walk in between the people heading towards us in case any of them were interested in petting me, giving me a treat, or praising me.

If we went to the dog park, I would go around to all of the people to let them know I was there.

However, I always set healthy boundaries. I knew what I was willing to accept and what I was not. I would get on mom's bed at night while she was brushing her teeth, and whatever else she had to do to get ready to go to sleep, but when she came in the bedroom to get in bed, I would jump down and get into my own bed for sleeping. I needed my space to sleep peacefully. I couldn't have her accidentally brushing me with her foot if she moved in the night. In the morning, I would jump back up to let her know it was time for my breakfast. She'd try to make me cuddle, but that's not why I was up there—I had only one thing on my mind, and that was food!

Occasionally one of the cats, or even Mom, would try to sit on my bed with me. If it was one of the cats and they stayed far enough away to not touch me, I'd let them stay for a while. If Mom was feeling sad and needed some comforting, I'd let her stay for a bit too. It made her happy to rub the spot on my paws below the main pad – she said it was super soft. She also liked to touch my silky ears. But, if she was fine and just doing it to hassle me, then I'd grumble at her. It was MY bed after all.

At the dog park, I did not appreciate it when another dog would try to sniff my butt. I could do it to them if I wanted to, but it was not okay for them to do it back. I was not interested in letting them get to know me in that way. If they wanted to run around a bit with me, that was okay but stay out of my personal space!

Sometimes people aren't good at saying no or setting boundaries. They let people do whatever they want, even if it makes them uncomfortable or unhappy. Not me! I was clear on what I would accept and what I wouldn't. Humans seem to worry too much about what other people think. But it's perfectly acceptable to tell someone when they've breached your personal space. Be clear about what you need. It's not rude, it's self-care!

Get Plenty of Sleep and Stretch When You Rise

"Our minds must have relaxation: rested, they will rise up better and keener."
—Lucius Annaeus Seneca

H ave you ever noticed that dogs can sleep pretty much anywhere and anytime? That's because we don't worry about things we can't control. We don't hold grudges – in fact, we're quick to forgive. We also know the value of sleep.

Humans tend to sacrifice sleep for other things they think are important or have trouble sleeping when they can't turn off their minds. But sleep is one of the most important factors for well-being. Humans need anywhere from seven to nine hours of quality sleep per night to keep their bodies and minds healthy.

I loved heading to my bed when the day was over. I would snore the night away and stretch upon waking in the morning. My slumber gave me the energy I needed to do all of my favorite things during the day. After a play session, it's important to take a nap (especially for youngsters). Sometimes when you're trying to work something out or solve a problem, a nap is the best thing you can do. I like to say, "When in doubt, take a nap!"

The body needs rest for recovery, so it's especially important to get plenty of sleep when you're not feeling well or are healing from an injury. Sleep is essential for physical and mental well-being, as well as for your overall health. Sleep allows your body and mind to recharge, leaving you refreshed and alert when you wake up.

Sometimes Mom would work even when she had a bad cold. Then she wondered why that cold held on for weeks at a time. I could have told her it was because she wasn't getting enough rest to help her immune system fight off the virus. She thought that working from home meant that she could keep working even when she should have called out sick to take care of herself. What she needed to do was stop doing and get some sleep!

There's not much that cats do better than dogs, but I have to hand it to them, they really value their sleep. Kali and Mateo slept even more than I did during the day.

Napping is one of Kali's favorite pastimes, and she particularly liked curling up underneath a blanket on the couch and staying there for hours at a time. I suppose they probably got up earlier than me, but I'm sure they spent more hours sleeping than anyone else in the house.

Speaking of things that are good for you—stretching is also important. I enjoyed doing my neck stretches while sitting in the lawn chair in the backyard. I would lift my muzzle towards the sky and work any kinks out of my neck. I did plenty of what Mom calls "downward dog pose" to stretch my spine and keep my back healthy and limber.

Consider what impacts your sleep or keeps you from getting at least seven hours of sleep a night. Make sleep a priority by setting a reminder for the time you need to head to bed to get enough hours before you have to be up in the morning. Better yet, get a dog. I always let Mom know when it was time for our night-time routine of going outside, having a treat, and then climbing into bed. I went to bed without her if she wasn't listening.

Notice how much better you feel throughout the day after getting a decent night's sleep. If you experience that afternoon slump, settle in for a short (fifteen-to-twenty-minute) nap. And don't forget to stretch when you get up. Your body will thank you.

Shake It Off

"Shake it off and bounce back."
—Unknown

Long before the Taylor Swift song *Shake It Off* came along, dogs were doing just that. Dogs have the innate wisdom that our bodies hold onto emotions. Of course, we shake for other reasons too—like if we're wet. Science has found dogs can shake 70% of the water from our fur in only four seconds. Pretty impressive, right? But you've probably noticed that we shake sometimes even if we're dry.

If we are stressed, for example, if we just had a tussle with another dog, we take a moment to shake our entire bodies to get that emotion out, and to take a timeout. Shaking is a way of releasing both tense muscles and tense emotions. This means we might also "shake it off" after intense excitement—like after greeting our humans when they get home by zooming around the house or yard. The "shake-off" is like a reboot.

After waking from sleep, we might shake to get ready for action. It's like your morning cup of coffee—the shake-off helps prepare us for the day ahead. Scientists attribute this to a survival instinct from when our ancestors had to sleep on the ground. They shook off upon waking to clear their fur of anything that gathered or got stuck there while they were asleep. Shaking off sleep is also a way to get rid of any feelings of discomfort after having been in the same position for a while. I preferred to stretch over shaking it off after sleep.

Humans can benefit from the shake-off, too. When you hold onto physical tension, it can cause your muscles to stiffen, which can lead to soreness. Maybe even more importantly, the body holds onto emotional tension, and over time that can lead to chronic conditions or issues. Shaking it off allows you to get it out of your system so you can move on.

Have you ever noticed that when you dance, it makes you feel happier? It could be because you are moving your body in that way allows you to release some tension.

Mom loved dancing, especially in the kitchen while making dinner. When we lived in Broomfield, Mom would go to a class at the fitness center after work called Dance Jam. It involved doing choreographed dances to popular hip-hop songs. She was always in the best mood when she got home from that class. I can totally understand why—she was "shaking it off!" Later, when we moved to a house that was an hour away from that gym, she was still able to do the routines because the teacher had posted many of them on YouTube. I know it wasn't the same for her as going in person, but it still made her happy.

Hydrate

"Water is like oil for your body's engine.
Keep it lubricated and running
smoothly."
—Unknown

I spent my life in Colorado where the air is really dry. The two places we lived at were at about 5,500 feet and 8,000 feet above sea level. That's high! There's not much humidity in the air and with 300 days of sunshine per year, not a lot of rain. That all meant I needed to drink a lot of water to stay hydrated.

Mom sometimes called me a camel, because I would be at the water bowl for a while, drinking up as much as I could. They say that once you feel thirsty, you're already dehydrated, so I made sure it didn't come to that. Mom brought a collapsible bowl with us on hikes so if there wasn't a creek or river nearby the trail, she could share water with me from her bottle. We would take breaks along the way, especially during the summer, and I would take a long drink (after getting my treat, of course).

I don't know all of the science, but according to the people at the Mayo Clinic (thanks to Mom for looking this up):

Every cell, tissue, and organ in your body needs water to work properly. For example, water:

- Gets rid of wastes through urination, perspiration, and bowel movements
- Keeps your temperature normal
- Lubricates and cushions joints
- Protects sensitive tissues[1]

Even mild dehydration can drain your energy and make you tired. That's not good. There's so much adventuring to do, and you need energy to fuel you.

Mom drank a lot of water and had either a hydration backpack or a reusable water bottle with her on hikes. At home, she kept a glass of water on her desk while she worked and would get up to refill as needed. It meant we both had to take breaks to pee frequently, but it's better than being dehydrated.

The only thing I drank was water. Mom would drink other things, including alcohol. I'm not sure why because that stuff is poison. She would sometimes let me sniff her beer or glass of wine, but I would turn up my nose and pull away. It didn't smell good at all, and I'm sure it tasted even worse. I'm not sure why she bothered drinking it. Sometimes she would have too much and spend part of the next day feeling awful. I would think she would have learned her lesson, but it happened more than once. Luckily, it usually made her feel better to get outside, so after laying on the couch for a bit, she'd grab my leash and we'd go out for a walk. The fresh air seemed to make it better.

I recommend you stick with water. It's much better for you. Mala learned from me and was good at hydrating. We both liked to drink from the same bowl, and the cats did too, so that bowl had to get refilled a lot. Kali (the cat who thought I was her best friend) was particular about the water in the bowl. If it got some dirt or hair in it, she'd paw at it until Mom would notice what a mess she was making and dump it out to replace it with fresh water. It's good to keep water around so you have it available when you need it. Don't leave home without your reusable water bottle or bowl.

Live in the Present Moment. And Be Curious About the World Around You.

"Man postpones or remembers: he does not live in the present, but with reverted eye laments the past, or, heedless of the riches that surround him, stands on tiptoe to foresee the future. He cannot be happy and strong until he too lives with nature in the present, above time."
—Ralph Waldo Emerson

Humans tend to spend a lot of time thinking about the past or worrying about the future. Dogs live in the present moment. We're great at engaging with the world around us and giving our full attention to what is happening right here, right now.

Whenever I got into the trash and emptied it all over the floor, I wasn't worried about the consequences, I was focused on seeing what I could find. Usually, there wasn't that much of interest, but I went through every bit of it to pull out any tasty morsels that were hiding in there. I particularly liked used tissues, which Mom thought was gross, but I found delicious. Mom would get pretty mad at me when she got home from work and found garbage all over the place. I knew she wasn't going to like it, so I would stand at the lowest level of our tri-level house and grin at her (showing as many teeth as I could), begging for forgiveness. She would be mad for a few minutes while she cleaned up the mess, but she always forgave me. Hiding the trash bin in the cabinet under the kitchen sink was not enough to keep me out of it, so eventually she started storing it in the garage. That was the end of my daily treasure hunt. I always took any chance I could get to cruise through a trash bin I could access when we went somewhere.

On walks and hikes, I was fully engaged in the world around me—always on the lookout for animals, birds, interesting scents, discarded food, or people who might want to say hello to me. I would often stop to investigate further if something caught my attention. I stopped to take in the views, especially in my favorite spots, or when we traveled to new places. I think one of my favorite views was when we drove the Going-to-the-Sun road in Glacier National Park in Montana. Dad put my window down so I could look out at the amazing views while we were driving. They call Montana 'Big Sky Country' for a reason. The views are incredible, and worth the time to pause and take in, rather than rushing on by.

As Gene Baur put it in his book *Farm Sanctuary: Changing Hearts and Minds About Animals and Food*, animals are "always engaged in the world around them…They are connected to the physical world in a way that humans seem to have lost…animals show us the enjoyment of simple pleasures and of being in the moment."[1]

When Mom started practicing yoga, she used meditation to get more present. She would sit on her meditation pillow with our cat, Mateo, in her lap, close her eyes, and be silent for ten to twenty minutes. She got into the habit of doing this regularly, and it seemed to help her. She slowed down, was more relaxed, and didn't let work get her as upset. That benefited all of us. When she finally decided to leave her corporate job in 2018 to focus solely on running her own business, she had a lot more time to go on long walks with me. We even started going on hikes during the week.

Being more present meant that Mom was also paying more attention to what was going on with her body. It was about time because she hadn't done a good job of that before. One day when she was thirty-one years old, she had a heart attack while she was out for a bike ride. If her friend hadn't been with her, Mom wouldn't have gone to the hospital, and I would have been left all alone: the doctor told her she wouldn't have survived if she hadn't gone to the hospital that night. I was really worried when she unexpectedly didn't come home for three days, and I was left in the care of one of her friends. Finally, on the fourth day, her friend took me to the hospital where I could visit with her. Mom seemed okay by then, and boy was I glad! We had so much more adventuring to do together!

Eat Fruits and Vegetables

"You are what you eat. Choose fruits and vegetables to nourish your body and fuel your energy."
—Unknown

I know what you're thinking – this is an odd topic for a dog. Many people think dogs are carnivores, but that's cats. Dogs are omnivores. We eat all kinds of things ... including, in my case, things I really shouldn't. But I did know that fruits and vegetables are good for you (for the most part–there are a few things dogs shouldn't eat, like grapes, for example).

Mom made green juice most weekday mornings. She would go into the kitchen and pull out a bunch of vegetables, an apple, and a lime, rinse them, cut them up, and run them through her juicer. As she was prepping everything, she would give me bites of each thing. I liked carrots the most. I would eat celery and sometimes the apple she gave me (although I preferred the red ones and she always used green apples for making juice). I usually turned down the kale, although later in life, I realized that was pretty good, too. When Mala came into the family, she started joining me for this morning ritual. She seemed to like almost all vegetables, except for plain lettuce. Mom called Mala her "veggie girl." That made me a little jealous, so I started accepting even more vegetables (even those green apples and kale).

As someone who thinks what you eat is the most important factor for your health, Mom is a big proponent of eating more vegetables. She always says most people don't eat enough leafy greens and that everyone can use more fiber in their diet. Mom was extra passionate about eating healthy after her heart attack. The doctors wanted her to take pharmaceuticals for the rest of her life to keep her cholesterol extra low to help prevent another heart attack, but she didn't like that idea. After she read a lot about plant-based diets, she started transitioning away from eating any animal products.

Mom eating more plants meant I also ate more plants. She even put me on vegan dog food for a bit, but I didn't love it, so she switched me back to regular food. But she kept eating less and less animal products and eventually was about 99% vegan. She loved the Italian dessert tiramisu, so she would have that every once in a while. I can't blame her—Italians have the best foods! She stopped taking prescription medicine and managed to still keep her cholesterol low enough to be in the least-risk category of having another heart event. I was proud of her for taking care of her body because I wanted her to stick around.

I'm not saying you have to go fully plant-based like Mom, but I do think everyone can benefit from eating more fruits and vegetables. Mom met with most of her health coaching clients via Zoom, so I often heard her sharing the benefits of eating whole, plant-based foods. They have a lot of nutrients that your body needs to stay healthy and strong. Fruits and vegetables are rich in nutrients, fiber, potassium, and antioxidants that can help you fend off inflammation, lower your blood pressure, and protect your eyes, skin, and most importantly, your heart. It's best to get nutrients from an actual whole food rather than trying to supplement. So, my advice: include things like berries, kale, and carrots in your meals. Your body will thank you.

A Dog Might Be Man's Best Friend, but a Kid Is a Dog's Best Friend

"No man is complete until he has owned a dog. And a dog is complete only when it has had a boy."
—Unknown

My love for kids started with a neighbor's little girl. When Mom had to go out of town, the neighbors would bring me to their house to hang out with them and their two dogs. I didn't always get along well with the older dog, but I enjoyed hanging out with that little human. After the first time they had me over, the little girl told Mom that I was her dog, because I chewed up one of her Barbie dolls. Mom was horrified

that I ruined her toy, but the little girl didn't mind at all—
I was pure joy to her.

I liked most kids. Once when we were out
snowshoeing, we came across a family who was pulling
their toddler in a sled. I saw my chance! I immediately got
into the sled and started licking that kid's face and hands
hoping for sticky fingers from breakfast. Mom was
worried the parents would be mad, but they thought it was
funny, and the kid loved the attention I gave her.

Another day—at the dog park—I saw a little kid
running around the fenced-in area and got excited since I
love to run. I started running after her. It was so much fun
that I got a little too excited and ended up knocking the
girl down. She was fine, and her parents accepted that
when you bring your kid to a dog park something like that
is bound to happen, so I didn't get into trouble. Mom just
told me I had to be more careful.

During our walks in the neighborhood, we'd often
come across kids who wanted to pet me, and I happily
accepted. On one particular day, there was a group of
about eight kids. Mala was with us at the time, and she
gave the group a wide berth because she felt the exact
opposite as I do about kids. I gladly stood right in the
middle of that group and let them fawn over me for as
long as they wanted. It also allowed me to see if any of
them had some food I could easily remove from their little

hands. As the saying goes, "as easy as taking candy from a baby."

Mom and Dad never had kids, which was a bit of a disappointment for me, but at least I didn't have to share their attention with a human baby. After all, I was their child, and I loved it. I had plenty of interactions with children, so it was okay I didn't live with one.

People always say a dog is man's best friend, and that's true, but kids are definitely a dog's best friend. They're at our level, and in their innocence, they love more like we do—completely and unconditionally. Most children are kind and compassionate towards animals, which isn't always the case for adults. Kids also tend to be generous with doling out treats. What's not to love?

Take Your Job Seriously, but Make Time for Fun

I was head of security for our family, and I took my job seriously since day one. I spent lots of time in the backyard, patrolling the fence, barking at the elementary school kids who were out at recess in the field that backed up to our fence, and fighting with the red squirrel who loved to run along the top of the fence and climb the branches of our trees. That squirrel provoked me by chattering at me—the nerve!

Our backyard had a big green neighborhood electrical box. It turned out to be the perfect height for me to stand on so I could put my paws on top of the fence to see everything that was happening behind the house. If a dog happened to be walking along the street a block over on the path that came around to our neighborhood, I was sure to let them know they were intruding on my territory! My other backyard post was the lawn chair, which I climbed into when I wasn't patrolling the fence.

I didn't appreciate much about our cat, Kali (who, as I may have mentioned, seemed quite smitten with me), but I did respect her ability to climb trees and walk along the top of the fence. Kali was referred to as Tower Two because she provided our security team with a bird's-eye view.

When I wasn't out in the yard, I was in the recliner by the picture window in the front of the house, watching for the suspicious man in the brown truck who dared to drop things off at our front door.

While I was a medium-sized dog (about fifty pounds), my bark was that of a much larger, more intimidating dog. When my favorite neighbors moved out (the ones with the little girl who loved me), the guy who bought their house was not my favorite. Sometimes when Mom was traveling and a pet sitter was staying with me, I'd go out into the backyard at 5:00 p.m. to announce to the neighborhood that I hadn't received my dinner yet. The new neighbor would call the police when that happened, which made me bark even more because they would park in front of the house, and sometimes a person in uniform would come to the front door.

Mom was pretty mad when she found out she had a criminal record because of that neighbor. She didn't read the fine print on the $50 ticket she paid when she got back from her work trip that paying the fine meant admitting guilt to a misdemeanor "disturbing the peace–barking dog." She worked hard and didn't have time for the alternative, which was to go to court. It wasn't until a prospective employer ran a background check that Mom learned about her record. Luckily, they hired her anyway.

When we moved to a one-and-a-half-acre lot in the mountains, my parents said I could retire from my security job, but I worked right up until the day I couldn't go outside on my own anymore. I chased chipmunks and gave that man in the brown truck a piece of my mind when he had the nerve to breach my perimeter. Mala didn't bark much when I was still around, but I taught her everything I knew, and after I left my Earthly body, I was proud to look down and see she had picked up right where I left off. She gets even more upset at that man with the brown truck than I did!

Even though I took my job seriously, I always made time for fun. I enjoyed my daily walks, weekend hikes, and, as I mentioned earlier, playing with my squeaky toys when I was younger. Playing fetch was silly—why would I keep bringing it to you, if you're just going to throw it again? However, I did have fun running around in the field behind the house or at the park down the road.

I helped Mom make time for fun too. She worked long hours sometimes but would always make sure to take me for a walk or jog daily. It got her off her computer and outside in nature where she could relax and have a bit of fun. While it's good to be proud of your work, it's important to not let it define who you are. You are so much more than your job title. Be sure to explore what makes you feel alive and make time for that every day.

Care More, Do Better

"In nature we never see anything isolated, but everything in connection with something else which is before it, beside it, under it and over it."
—Johann Wolfgang von Goethe

There are billions of animals, plants, and humans sharing this one Earth. Just by living, we are using resources that will no longer be available to those who come after us. That doesn't mean we shouldn't do our best to take care of the planet for future generations. The whole world benefits if we each do our small part to care more and do better.

As a dog, I didn't have a lot of control over my "carbon footprint," but I was glad to have parents who do their best to treat others (all beings) and the Earth with care. We lived fairly simply. Mom tried not to accumulate too much "stuff." She had a lot of hobbies, so she did own things that allowed her to do the things she loved (like bikes, a kayak, and a paddle board), but she didn't put a lot of value on material things. Her brother used to tease her that the TV in our house was smaller than his computer monitor, but it didn't bother her. We liked to have experiences more than possessions.

While Mom transitioned to eating mostly plant-based to protect her heart health, she also did it so that she wasn't contributing to the harm to animals and the planet that occurs in animal agriculture. She was really worried about the harm caused by growing feed for animals versus growing plants people can eat directly. A lot of land and water is tied up in animal agriculture. There are also a lot of chemicals used in conventional farming that harm the soil, so she bought local and organic when possible.

Mom didn't like having to use so many plastic bags to clean up my poop on walks and hikes, but there weren't a lot of alternatives. She did manage to find some compostable bags so she could clean up after me without using so much plastic. She also reused and recycled what she could. Mom avoided using single-use produce bags and grocery bags. She got glass containers for leftover food.

Mom even tried her hand at growing some of her own food. Her garden didn't do that great, but she did her best. I enjoyed the cherry tomatoes she grew in pots in the backyard. I also thought the corn she grew was delicious, but she wasn't amused that I ate most of it before she could pick the cobs. I thought it was all up for grabs since it was in the backyard, which, let's be honest, was my territory. Mala liked the cucumbers. Mom got mad at her when she picked the first one of the season, so when Mala picked the second one, she took just one bite and then brought the rest of it to Mom for her to eat. Before another one could grow, Mala pulled the whole plant out of the ground, so that was the end of the cucumbers.

Some people don't seem to care that they're consuming at a rate that is using up precious resources and harming the planet. I think that if you can do better, you should try. We all need to care about the impact our actions have on those around us. We only have this one Earth, and she needs to be treated with respect. We can't just take, take, take, without pausing to think about how we can ensure there's enough for everyone.

Take the Road Less Traveled

"Two roads diverged in a wood, and I—
I took the one less traveled by,
And that has made all the difference."
—Robert Frost
(from The Road Not Taken)

I wasn't your typical dog, and I didn't do things the same way as other dogs. I liked to take the road less traveled. I was clear about what I loved to do and made sure Mom knew what I wanted. When we went for walks, I would often pull in the direction that would result in a longer outing. On hikes, I liked to explore areas where I could climb on the rocks and sniff out critters. I taught Mala to do that, too, when she came into our family. She was an even better rock climber than me! I was surprised by some of the places she could get.

When we first met, Mom worked for a big company in a job that I'm sure was important but didn't make her happy. After she survived the heart attack she started thinking about changing paths. Mom was caught up in society's expectations of her—she thought that having a high-paying job and a mortgage were the symbols of her success.

Lucky for both of us, her near-death experience opened her eyes to the fact that she wasn't living her purpose. She was simply going through the motions. Mom was on the road expected of her, but it wasn't fulfilling. Mom worked in Human Resources, which is what she had gone to college for, so she wasn't sure what else to do. All I knew was that she shouldn't be working so many hours. That prevented us from being able to go on as many adventures as we both desired.

Mom started taking classes in nutrition, health coaching, and yoga. Eventually, she was certified to start coaching people and teaching yoga. She was still working full-time in her other job when she started her own business. Mom wasn't sure she could make enough money teaching yoga and helping people get healthy to keep a roof over our heads and food in our bowls, but she sure was happier when she was working on her own business.

Mom finally got to a place where she was able to go part-time at her HR job. About a year after that, she finally left the corporate job to focus full-time on running her own company. She still got stressed from time to time, but at least she got the satisfaction of doing something she felt made a difference in the lives of others.

In life, you could do the things that are going to earn you money or prestige, but if those things don't allow you to share your unique gifts, then is it really worth it? There's only one of you, and the world needs the special gift only you have. So, ask yourself, what makes the time fly by when you're doing it? What brings you joy? Is there something that others need that overlaps with what you love doing? If so, maybe give it a shot. It might be a different path than the one you're currently on, or from what others expect you to do, but why spend your life on the road that isn't for you?

Trust Your Instincts

---

*"There is a voice that doesn't use words.
Listen."*
—Rumi

Dogs are good at following our hunches. People tend to get too caught up in their thoughts and don't listen to their hearts. They forget that the truth lies in what they feel in their gut. We all have inner wisdom and already know the right answer. Humans spend too much time doubting their intuition.

I knew to approach with caution if a dog or person didn't seem friendly. I was good at reading others. If I got a bad vibe, I steered clear or gave a warning bark to keep them away from me. I especially did this when I was walking with Mom because it was my job to protect her. She told me I didn't need to worry, that she could take care of herself, but I wasn't so sure. I felt compelled to scare away anyone who seemed like a threat.

I talked about my survival skills already. If I heard a storm rolling in, I would seek shelter. The bathtub was a great place to hang out during a thunderstorm. You never know what can happen, so it's best to be safe. I knew nothing could get me if I was in the bathtub or underneath the bed—including whatever was going to follow that terrible beeping sound the smoke detectors made sometimes.

One smoke detector located on the vaulted ceiling above the stairs in our house in Broomfield was hard to reach. Mom owned a fancy ladder you could set up in multiple ways, including on the stairs. However, she did not like ladders and wouldn't stand on the highest rung for fear of falling, which was smart. One night that hard-to-reach smoke detector started to beep telling us the battery was low. It was driving me crazy, and Mom knew neither of us would sleep that night if she couldn't get it to stop beeping. She couldn't reach it on her own, even with the ladder. Mom grabbed the broom and smacked that smoke detector until she got it to release and fall. That took care of that. I appreciated she didn't want me to suffer all night with that annoying beeping sound. She was a champion. But I digress, let's get back to instincts.

Mom liked having me around, especially when we lived alone. I made her feel more secure. We hiked a lot, and Mom felt safer being out in the woods with me by her side. I could keep my eyes and ears open for any potential threats. A dog can alert you to anything that's coming because we can already sense or hear it before it's audible to you. Colorado does have bears and mountain lions. We did see bears while out on the trails, but never a mountain lion. That doesn't mean they weren't there, but if they were, they kept their distance.

I suppose dogs have more finely tuned instincts than people do, or we just don't get as distracted by outside factors. Having a dog around can help you get in touch with your connection to the natural world, and to your instincts. Mom used to question her intuition a lot. She got caught up in thinking about everything a bit too much. She spent so much time being logical that she lost touch with what her heart was trying to tell her. It's no surprise it was her heart that finally got her attention.

After Mom survived that heart attack, she started meditating so she could slow down her thoughts, reconnect to her gut instincts, and find out what her heart needed so it could stay healthy.

Even though it wasn't the most logical choice (in some people's view), Mom's decision to leave her corporate job to follow her heart was the right one for her. Through her own business, she helps others on their paths to happier, healthier lives. Mom leads yoga retreats all over the world, teaches wellness workshops, and coaches people to build healthy habits. I'm proud she stopped getting so caught up in her mind and finally followed her heart.

Ella meets her new sister, Anabelle, in the backyard of her new home.

Ella claims the recliner by the front window as her chair.

Ella pauses to play with a pinecone during a hike.

Ella and Carrie pose at a winery in Colorado during one of many road trips.

Ella with her toys.

Ella and Carrie on a mountaintop in Colorado.

*Ella taking a break from her
security rounds of the yard.*

Ella always had a big smile when we were hiking.

Carrie and Ella enjoying a special moment together.

Ella and Mala served as ring bearers during our
wedding ceremony. Ella was disappointed not to be
allowed at the reception. Majesty Photo

Our cat, Kali, thought Ella was her best friend and always wanted to be near her.

Ella always looked out for her family, especially when we were in vulnerable positions like sitting or lying in the grass at the park.

*Ella started paddle boarding in
her later years and loved it.*

*Ella learned to get around using her Walkin' Wheels®
wheelchair when she could no longer move her back leg.*

*Ella still enjoyed paddle boarding up
until her final days.*

*On her last road trip, Ella loved walking along the rim
of the Grand Canyon and enjoying the ultimate vista.*

Protect Those You Love and Be Cautious of Those Who Are Out to Get You

"When you open your heart to a dog, you gain a protector for life. Their loyalty is their promise, their bravery their shield."
—Unknown

I took the job of protecting my family seriously. When I was walking with Mom, I always made sure that any dog that seemed aggressive couldn't get too close. I would bark my deep, scary bark. I wasn't the type to bite, but I made sure they knew I was tough. Sometimes Mom thought I went a little overboard, and she would distract me with treats as other dogs were going by.

When I got older, Mom finally trusted me enough to come when she called me, so she took a class to earn a special tag for me. The tag allowed me to be off-leash on certain trails. When I was off leash, I was off duty and didn't have to worry as much about her well-being. I would go a little bit ahead, but never out of sight. I would stop and look back to be sure Mom was still coming and hadn't gotten lost or anything. I didn't feel the need to bark at other dogs when I was off leash since that meant I could simply roam and wasn't in charge of protecting anyone. This seemed to be a relief for Mom.

I already told you about my job as head of security for the house, but that sometimes extended to other areas. When we went to the park, Mom would sometimes lie down in the grass. That seemed like a vulnerable position for her to be in as she wouldn't be able to see if someone was coming towards her, so I would stand guard. I stood over her, usually by her head since that was where I could be closest. She thought it was cute; I just thought it was practical and safe. I couldn't have her being so open to attack or surprise.

When I was an only child, I would just wander around at the dog park to take in all of the smells. When Mala joined our family, I had to start paying close attention at the dog park. If another dog started bullying her, I'd be there in a flash to let them know that if they wanted to mess with her, they had to go through me. The only dog allowed to wrestle with her was me. I couldn't trust those other dogs wouldn't hurt her. I might not have chosen to have a little sister, but once I did, it was my responsibility to protect her.

That applied to everyone in our family. It's important to be able to read people and other dogs to know who you can allow near your loved ones, and who you should scare away. As I mentioned earlier, I knew the neighbor who moved in next door, didn't like me, so I barked when I saw him outside the house. Mom said that didn't really help my case, and that barking at him only made it worse, but I didn't trust him. Our neighbors on the other side and across the street were great. When they had their garage doors open, I would go inside to look around. An open door is an invitation, after all. But Mom would always come get me and tell me not to be nosy. That seemed silly because I knew they were okay with me snooping around.

Some humans are better than others at reading people. Mom liked to believe most people have good intentions, so she was pretty trusting. That's why I felt the need to watch over her so much. Once Dad was around, I didn't have to worry as much, because he shared the duty of protecting her. But he would lie down in the grass sometimes too, so then I needed to stand guard over both of them. It's a good thing they had me around!

Life is an Adventure ...
Climb Aboard!

"If happiness is the goal — and it should be, then adventures should be top priority."
—Richard Branson

I was always up for an adventure from the beginning. I was lucky to be adopted by a person who loved adventure as much as I did. Mom worked a lot during periods of our time together, but she always made sure we got out to see the world as much as possible. When we only had a weekend, we mostly adventured on nearby trails in the foothills or lakes or reservoirs in the area. Mom was good about taking her vacation time, and I was thrilled when those weeks off included me. Sometimes she would have to fly to a far-off place, so I would either stay at home with a pet sitter or go to the farm that doubled as a boarding kennel.

Road trips were my favorite because we got to see places I hadn't been to before. We traveled all over the western United States together. Colorado is big and has a lot of great places to visit, and we explored as much of it as possible from the Eastern plains to the Southwest mountain towns. One of our first trips was when my grandparents and great-grandmother came all the way out to Colorado from New Hampshire to see me and Mom. We piled into Mom's Jeep Liberty and drove all over the state. We walked to the highest point in Rocky Mountain National Park, went to wine country, stopped by a huge lake, checked out Ouray (which had a somewhat intimidating statue of a mountain lion on Main Street that startled me when I first saw it), and drove up Pikes Peak. Not only was it a fabulous adventure, but my grandparents made sure I had all the treats I needed.

In addition to exploring Colorado, I traveled to Utah, Nevada, California, Wyoming, Montana, Idaho, New Mexico, and Arizona. I was completely fine with riding in the car for long hours so we could discover new places. I loved looking out over the ocean, mountains, and canyons that make the western part of the United States so beautiful.

I kept adventuring right up until the end, and I wouldn't have it any other way. As Hunter S. Thompson wrote in *The Proud Highway: Saga of a Desperate Southern*

Gentleman, 1955-1967, "Who is the happier man, he who has braved the storm of life and lived, or he who has stayed securely on shore and merely existed?"[1]

I know I'm lucky to have gotten to do so many things and travel to a lot of places. Some dogs live their lives fenced in or tied up in their yard and never get to go anywhere else. What a boring life that must be. People are lucky they have the freedom to go wherever they want. Not everyone takes advantage of those opportunities. I'm not sure why they don't; maybe some of it is fear of the unknown. Travel and adventure expand your horizons. You learn about yourself, and about how others live. Experiencing new places allows you to truly live, and not just exist.

It's no wonder that the people who don't open themselves up to adventure tend to feel a bit blah about life. A life of adventure is one of endless opportunity. The more you explore, the more of this great big world you experience, and the more you discover who you are and what makes you happy. If you're not happy, change something. Try something new. It doesn't have to be a big thing like traveling to a far-off place; it could be as simple as sitting in your backyard and admiring the way the leaves flutter in the breeze or listening to the chirp of a bird. Take off your shoes and feel the grass beneath your feet. Take a moment to see your space in a new way. Take your dog along. We're great at living life as though it's a grand adventure.

Be Kind, but Don't Be a Pushover

"No act of kindness, no matter how small, is ever wasted."
—Aesop

I might not have been the most outwardly affectionate dog. I gave love on my terms, but I was kind-hearted. It's important to be kind because you never know what someone else is going through or dealing with. Be kind, not to get something in return, but because it's the right thing to do. There's a lot of suffering in the world and being kind is a simple way to bring a little more compassion and joy to someone's day.

I was especially gentle with little kids. They're so innocent and, like animals, they have a pure heart. Children are kind and compassionate. I loved being around them and letting them pet me. Mom said I would have made a great therapy dog. She looked into it once, but the program at the local hospital wasn't accepting any more dogs at the time. It's too bad because I agreed with her. I would have been a great therapy dog!

While you need to be kind, you also need to stand up for yourself. You shouldn't let anyone boss you around. I've talked already about setting healthy boundaries. This is along that same vein. When we went to the dog park, the dogs who were already there would run over to greet me upon my arrival. I was fine with a quick hello, but if a dog lingered too long, I'd give them a warning bark and then run off to do the things I wanted to do. I spent most of my time checking out all the smells and visiting with the people who were there.

I was the same way on a hiking trail. If another dog got a little too much in my business, I would bark at them to indicate I wasn't having it. I was there to enjoy the great outdoors. Sometimes other dogs didn't like that I barked at them, and they'd bark back. Mom would pull me along and tell me not to worry about it, to stay calm. I felt I needed to give them a piece of my mind, so when I was young, I didn't always give up so easily. Eventually, I saw Mom's point that it wasn't worth all the fuss and would trot along with her after just one or two barks.

When Mala came along, I took it upon myself to make sure no one messed with her. If she found herself surrounded by some dogs at the park whose intentions didn't seem pure, I'd run over and give them a piece of my mind. She was my little sister and the only one who could tell her what to do was me! While I was kindhearted, Mala was a saint (if a little naive). She seemed to believe all dogs were nice and would run up to any dog at any time. This resulted in her getting bit in the face once, but that didn't seem to faze her. Mala was full of love, and the people upon whom she lavished her love the most were our parents. I was happy she would be there to comfort them after I passed. I knew Mom would really need it.

Mom was one of the most kind-hearted people I ever met. She loved all animals; she would even rescue insects that got stuck in some water and couldn't get out. She was nice to people, too, and would seek ways to help others who needed it. She donated blood regularly, made lots of donations to charitable organizations, and gave out supplies to homeless people. When we walked around Dad's apartment in Denver (before he moved in with us), we would come across a lot of people who lived on the streets. I always wanted to say hello to them, so Mom would let me go over and greet them. I think it made them happy to pet me.

I found that when you're kind to others, they're more likely to be kind in return. By living life with a kind heart, you make the world a more compassionate place. There's a lot of pain in the world, and anything each one of us can do to make the world a little brighter is worth the effort. If someone takes advantage of your kindness, be sure to let them know you're not okay with that. As I mentioned before, having healthy boundaries is good for your well-being.

Walking is Good for Your Health and Happiness (Body, Mind, and Spirit)

"Walking is man's best medicine."
—Hippocrates

I loved going for walks, and sometimes I took myself if Mom wasn't ready to take me. When she opened the front door, I'd slip out and head for the path around the pond. By the time Mom got some shoes on, grabbed a leash, and caught up with me, I was halfway around the pond. I knew the way—we took that path all the time!

I didn't need a leash, but Mom did. I had to lead the way so she wouldn't get lost. When I was a puppy and getting used to the leash, it would always pull on my neck. I finally figured out the exact length of the leash at its longest point (it was retractable), so I could stay at the farthest possible distance without it pulling on my neck.

I knew all our usual walking routes, including the places where we had to decide between a short loop or an extended walk. Whenever we got to one of those points, I would pull in the direction that would result in the longest walk. Sometimes Mom acquiesced if it was a nice day, but other times, if she needed to get to work, she would lead me back the short way.

My parents thought they were pretty funny, saying I always wanted to take the long way because I needed to walk my full territory to check on my subjects and give them a chance to see and honor their ruler—I was the Queen after all. But really, I just loved to walk. I had a lot of nicknames, some of which were silly (what exactly is an "L Bean" or a "Doogle?"), but I was fine with being called Queen Ella.

When Mom and Dad first adopted Mala, she didn't know what to think of the leash. When they attached the leash to her collar she would sit down and not want to walk. I showed her the ropes though, and before long we were all walking around the neighborhood together.

Later in life, when that nasty degenerative myelopathy claimed my back right leg, I could no longer go on my daily walks unassisted. I had to finally accept the Walkin' Wheels® device Mom had bought for this purpose. At first, I scoffed at it because I didn't need it—I could still walk on my own, even though I was a little unsteady. But, once I realized the battle was lost and I couldn't make my right leg move anymore, I begrudgingly accepted being strapped into the wheels.

Once I got the hang of my wheels, I proudly strutted my stuff all over town, and even along the rim trail of the Grand Canyon. As a bonus, my wheels drew attention and praise from those who saw me. It was about time since after that fluffy little puppy Mala came into my life, she tended to get all of the attention, even though I would walk in between people who were coming towards us on the trail to be sure they noticed me. Everyone fawned over Mala when she was a puppy, and we couldn't go anywhere without having to stop so they could pet her. Now and then, a smart person would say hi to me too. But with those wheels, I was once again the center of attention, and I soaked up every second of it.

I'm not sure how many miles I walked throughout my life, but I'm sure it was significant. It kept me healthy in mind, body, and spirit. When Mom was working a lot, I could see her shoulders relax within minutes of taking me on my daily walk. I knew it helped her, so I always reminded her to lace up her shoes and get outside with me no matter how busy she was. She told me that walking helped her think more clearly.

You don't need any special equipment to walk – just a pair of shoes if you're a human. You can walk anywhere you are, provided it's not dangerous. You don't have to walk fast or far. There's no better way to brighten your day than to get outside. If you have the opportunity to walk in nature, even if it's just a few trees or shrubs, that's even better. If you engage all your senses, a walk turns into a sort of meditation and can ease your worries and relax your nervous system.

If you're lucky enough to have a dog, take them along. They will appreciate that time with you! It's healthy for us as dogs to get out and sniff, since we explore the world primarily through our sense of scent. Experiencing different smells stimulates our minds, and walking keeps our bodies healthy too. It's a win-win!

Live Your Passion: Never Stop Doing What You Love

"Your heart is a hidden treasure, Seek diligently and find out what it is."
—Rumi

I had endless energy most of my life. My three favorite activities to burn off some of that energy were running, hiking, and walking. I talked about my neighborhood strolls already and will tell you more about hiking soon, so I'll focus on my biggest passion: running.

Lucky for me Mom was a runner. Soon after she adopted me, she began training for a half-marathon, and during many of our years together she competed in triathlons. I know I wasn't always the easiest to jog with, because I tended to ping pong back and forth on the trail following my nose to all the best smells or trying to chase after those pesky prairie dogs. Sometimes I would cross right in front of Mom, causing her to have to stop on a dime. I was always on the lookout for fresh goose poop, which was plentiful on our favorite running trail since it went around a pond. I also liked to take a quick stop in the pond to cool off.

I didn't bother much with other dogs when we were jogging, because I was too busy having a good time. I did nearly dislocate Mom's shoulder a few times going after a rabbit that crossed the trail in front of us, or those chirping prairie dogs who would egg me on and then disappear into their holes. We saw coyotes a few times on our early morning runs, so Mom would shorten up my leash to keep me close and out of harm's way.

We had several routes from our house, some with nice stops built in, like the dog park. We would run the two miles there, then I would sniff around in the park, and visit with the people who were there (not the dogs though—I didn't have much interest in them, since it's not like they could pet me or give me any treats). After I grew bored, we'd jog the two miles back home.

One summer, when she was jogging a lot, Mom took me on an eight-mile run. Mom thought that would tire me out, but I was still ready to play when we got home. I think she wished she could harness some of my energy for herself because she was pretty tired. It energized me to do what I loved.

I jogged with Mom well into my elder years. Even when I was thirteen years old, we would go for some short jogs around the pond. We were both a bit slower by then, but I still enjoyed getting out and trotting along the dirt trails, which were easier on Mom's knees than the concrete or paved paths. By then Dad and Mala were part of our family, and those youngsters would run ahead of us. We'd all meet back up at the trailhead. I didn't mind, it gave me some alone time with Mom.

I was always happy to go for a run, as my smile indicated. Even if we were doing my other favorite activity (hiking), if someone jogged by us, I would pick up the pace to a trot and look back at Mom to communicate, "Aren't you coming? This is so fun!"

Life is short, and tomorrows are never guaranteed, so you should do what makes you happy now, rather than putting it off until some time in the future. All you have is the present moment.

Mom knows all about not putting off what you love until tomorrow. After she survived her heart attack, I told you she realized the work that she spent so much time doing didn't fulfill her, and she started seeking out her passion. Now, she loves what she does, and is much happier as a result. She jokes that she is semi-retired, but she's doing something that fulfills her, so it no longer feels like work.

Humans tend to put things off, thinking they have plenty of time, but there is no magical time when everything will be different. As dogs, we know that life is short and that you need to live your passion now. As Brendan Burchard wrote in *The Motivation Manifesto* "Life's purpose is to *live*—to live freely, vibrantly, joyously, madly, consciously, lovingly, enthusiastically."[1] So, go ahead, find what makes you feel alive, and do it!

Set Your Sights on the Goal, but Take Time to Enjoy the Journey

"Wherever you go, go with all your heart."
—Johann Wolfgang von Goethe

From the beginning, I loved hiking. But despite being eager to summit, I took the time to stop and enjoy all the wonderful things along the way.

We hiked a lot! There were a lot of options nearby since we lived in the foothills of Colorado. One favorite was the South Mesa Trailhead just off Route 93 on the way to Boulder. There were multiple trail options – including some that were good for jogging. As a bonus, there was a creek at the end of our hike or jog where I could cool off and get a drink. The only things you had to watch out for were rattlesnakes. We did encounter one in the middle of the trail on one of our jogs. Luckily, a passerby gave Mom a heads-up that the snake was there because we might not have noticed it on our own until it was too late. Mom reined me in, and we gave the snake a wide berth as we passed it.

That was also the trail where I found a huge mound of fresh cow manure one day. When I first saw the cows themselves, I was cautious and went around them. While I was careful not to get too close to the cows, their poop was another story. It smelled so strong I just had to drop down and merrily roll in that fresh paddy. Mom didn't see it until after I was already rolling, so she couldn't stop me. I had a good amount of manure caked in my fur and collar, so we had to drive home with all the windows down. Mom couldn't stand the smell, but I was quite proud of myself until I had to get a bath in the backyard when we got home. In the end, the joy I got out of it was worth the bath at the end.

My favorite hike of all was Mount Sanitas in Boulder. We hiked and jogged there all the time. When we were living close to Boulder, we went at least once a week, so we got in tip-top shape and could summit quickly. Often, we would hike up the steep side of the trail, where my favorite vista was located. There, you could look out over the trail that came up the other side of the mountain. Without fail, I would stop at that spot and look out for a few moments before Mom could coax me to continue. Then we'd head to the top, have a drink of water and a snack, and jog down the other side of the mountain (the part that wasn't as steep).

I got it in my head that our routine on Sanitas was the way it should always be. When Mom took a hiatus from jogging and started making us hike up and back down the same side of the mountain, I didn't like it. Even though I could be off my leash on the trail, Mom would have to put me back on the leash when she started back down the same side to convince me to go with her. Mom called me stubborn, but I preferred doing a loop versus an out-and-back so I could check out both trails.

Our family road trip to Montana was as much for me as anyone else in the family since I loved hiking and vistas so much. We did a hike near Bozeman that had a steep ascent that was tough on all of us, but worth the views. The descent was the first time I noticed there was something weird going on with my back legs—they were crossing a lot and felt unsteady on the way down. But it didn't stop me from doing another eight-mile hike on that same road trip. My age was starting to slow me down, but I was still up for adventure. I did get pretty tired, so when we visited a lake the next day, I lay on my side, on the ground! Mom was so surprised I was lying in the dirt that she took a picture of me. I was just too tired to care about getting my fur dirty. I was exhausted, but happy.

After I left my Earthly body, Mom, Dad, and Mala went to Mount Sanitas and spread some of my ashes at my favorite vista. They said some nice words about me and left a rose for me. They'll always refer to that spot as "Ella's Vista."

People are pretty good at setting goals, but not as skilled at enjoying the journey. What you learn and experience on the way to your goal is just as important as achieving it. You might even find your goal changes due to new circumstances that come up along the way, causing you to pivot or change course. If you're only focused on the finish line, you miss a lot of wonderful things that make up your life, so don't forget to slow down and enjoy the journey!

Celebrate Your Accomplishments

"Magic is believing in yourself, if you can do that, you can make anything happen."
—Johann Wolfgang von Goethe

I loved to celebrate. Mom was great at rewarding me when I did tricks, or when I was a "good dog," and also to celebrate my milestones. Because I was found on the streets, my actual date of birth was unknown. I had an estimated birthday, but we usually would celebrate the entire month of January to cover our bases. Mom also celebrated her entire birthday month. We both loved birthdays! I loved them because I knew I would get special treats, we would do fun things, and I would receive extra attention. Mom knew the importance of appreciating each trip around the sun since she had almost died when she was thirty-one. Every day after that was a gift, and she made a big deal about birthdays. I certainly was on board with that because I loved being doted upon.

If you haven't already figured it out, I was one smart cookie. I knew what I needed to do to get praise. I was quick to run through the litany of tricks I knew would earn me my treat. I enjoyed being around people and was extra friendly so they would pet me. I also knew when I was going to get in trouble for something, so I would grin extra hard at Mom in the hopes I could win her over and she'd brush off whatever I had done to make her mad.

Dogs know that life is short and that you have to celebrate as much as possible. There's no sense putting off something special to some other time because that time may never come. It's good to set goals, but equally important to enjoy the milestones. The way I hiked—with my sights on the summit but taking time along the way to take in the views—was a good reminder to my parents that they should appreciate and recognize their accomplishments along the way to their ultimate goal. Celebrating when you achieve your goal is great, but it's just as important to notice and celebrate the milestones along the way. Who knows, your ultimate goal may change! Life is always throwing you curveballs, but each small step you take is moving you forward.

When Mom left her corporate job to start her own business, she had a hard time recognizing all the small steps she was accomplishing, because there was no one to give her a pat on the back, except her. Mom can be hard on herself and have extra high expectations. Dad helped her set up a system where she could visually see all of the progress she was making so that she would give herself the credit she deserved.

Setting big goals is great, but those are only achieved by taking one step at a time. When Mom was coaching others in achieving their health and wellness goals, she was great at helping them break down the ultimate goal into actionable steps that could be taken every day. She sometimes forgot that the same applied to her.

The more you achieve the small steps, the more likely you'll be motivated to keep going. Success begets more success. If you only care about the final destination, you might get frustrated at the time it takes to get there and lose your motivation. However, if you set incremental goals, and celebrate accomplishing them, your determination will grow, and before you know it, that thing that seemed so far off will finally be in sight.

Be Determined, and Don't Let a Setback Stop You

> "Success and fulfillment in life rests on the unflagging ability to get up, to be ourselves, to chase our dreams with fire each day, to keep willing ourselves to the next level of presence and performance and potential."
> —Brendon Burchard (from the book The Motivation Manifesto)

I had a healthy level of determination my whole life. Remember I told you about my love of hiking? While I did take my time to enjoy the journey along the way, I was determined to make it to the top no matter what.

Mom says I had summit fever. I never liked to turn around until we got to the top. If I could see the summit during the hike, I would pull Mom along until we reached it. This was particularly tough on Mom the day she took me up Quandary Peak (a 14,000+ foot mountain in Colorado). You could see the summit from early on in the hike, so I pulled almost the whole way. Mom got pretty tired, but I was having a blast.

One day when I was a bit older, Dad took me on a hike with Mala. He didn't intend for us to go all the way to the summit of Bear Peak, which was a pretty long, tough hike, but when we got to the saddle between Bear Peak and South Boulder Peak, I was not interested in turning around. Even when it got steep and Dad said we were getting low on water, I was determined to get to the top. Dad was probably a bit dehydrated after that hike because he gave Mala and me the rest of the water.

During one of our many hikes, I saw a critter go into a hole in a hillside. Mom kept calling to me to keep walking with her and her friend, but I was determined to get that critter. I was digging as fast as I could at the hole he had disappeared into, but Mom came and hooked my leash to my collar and pulled me out of there. What a bust—I could have had him! And, even if I couldn't have, it was fun trying. Mala caught a critter on the trail one day, but when Mom yelled at her to drop it, she did right away. I don't think she knew what to do with him. She was just as surprised as the rest of us that she managed to catch him. After she released the critter and he scurried off, I kept trying to find him. But, once again, Mom put my leash on and pulled me onward.

Throughout your life, you'll have roadblocks and challenges on your way to your goals, but it's important to not let a setback derail you. You must be determined so you can pick yourself up and keep going. Sure, you might need to rest a bit, or ask for some help, but if you want something badly enough, you have to keep trying until you get it.

When degenerative myelopathy took away the use of my back right leg, I didn't let that stop me from living. I got used to my Walkin' Wheels® device so I could still go on neighborhood patrols and hikes. I couldn't go as far as I used to, but I still got out in the world. Mom and Dad had to help me get outside when I had to go to the bathroom, but we all figured out the most efficient way to get those needs taken care of. I was determined right up until the end.

Be Yourself Without Apology ... but Be Adaptable

"To be yourself in a world that is constantly trying to make you something else is the greatest accomplishment."
—Ralph Waldo Emerson

W e're all unique and special and don't need to modify who we are just to make others comfortable. Emerson's words are ones I certainly lived by, as we all should. I knew exactly who I was, and no one was going to change me.

I didn't let anyone tell me who I should be. People might have seen me as just a dog, but I had every right to sit in chairs, stay in fancy hotels, and go on adventures. I loved people and spent more of my time with them than with other dogs.

Never let anyone, or society's expectations, stop you from becoming or being who you are—your true self. Know what you value and let those values guide you.

When something was important to me, I didn't budge. I protected my family, ate all the food I wanted, and spent my time walking, hiking, and running. I didn't bother with the things that didn't bring me joy, like playing fetch or wrestling with other dogs. Maybe, as a dog, some people expected me to like those things, but they weren't my jam.

On the other hand, you have to accept that change is inevitable, and be flexible on certain things. We have to be able to adapt and go with the flow of life, or else we get stuck. I always disliked baths, being brushed, and going to the vet, but I knew those weren't worth fighting against. I accepted that those weren't so bad and were ultimately good for me.

There were plenty of times in my life when I had to adapt to new circumstances. I was eight years old the year Mom added two kittens, the boyfriend who would become my dad, and Mala to our family—all within a year! Even though I was no longer the sole focus of Mom's attention, I knew having an expanded family was ultimately a good thing, and it was.

I adapted again when we moved to our new house in the mountains after I had spent most of my life in the suburbs. With more space to explore, more smells to check out, and wildlife all around, it was stimulating to be in this new place.

When I started going to physical therapy for my DM, I was fairly easygoing about it. There were certain things I wouldn't stand for, like lying on my side on command. I was also a bit sneaky about my time on the water treadmill—occasionally I would put my back feet on the sides that weren't moving to take a break. This would work briefly until Mom noticed and the therapist would make me start walking again.

Even with all of these adaptations, I remained who I was at the core. I knew the things that were important to me and didn't waiver when it came to those. I didn't always do what I was told, and some people might have labeled me a bad dog, but Mom appreciated my tenacity and independent spirit. She defended me to those who judged me and loved me exactly as I was. If someone wants to change you, they're not the right person for you.

When Mom went through yoga teacher training, she read a translation of the ancient text the *Bhagavad Gita*. When she started teaching yoga, she summarized one of the verses to use as a theme for class. She told her students "It's better to follow our own path, though done with mistakes, than to follow another's perfectly." I agree that it's best to always be yourself, even if it ruffles a few feathers.

You're Never Too Old to Learn New Tricks

People say you can't teach an old dog new tricks, but I'm proof that that saying is false. Before Mala joined our family, I never made an effort to catch food or treats that were tossed my way—I would just let them bounce off me and land on the floor. I didn't have any competition, so I knew I could eat whatever it was with no effort once it hit the floor. Mom thought that was kind of weird since I was so food-motivated, but why expend energy unnecessarily?

That all changed when Mala came into the family because *now* I had competition. If I let anything make it to the floor, there was a chance Mala would get it. Suddenly, I started snatching whatever was tossed my way. I caught pieces of ciabatta bread the most consistently of any food tossed my way. I loved bread, pasta, and pizza. I definitely was *not* gluten-free. Gluten is delicious!

I didn't start paddle boarding until I was nine years old. Mom decided to give me a try on her new board since they were taking Mala out. I took to it with no problem. I enjoyed being out on the water without having to be *in* the water. We did hear some thunder in the distance on our first outing, so that was when the fun ended, and we headed back to the safety of the shore and the car.

My favorite experiences on the water occurred once when we floated along on a gentle river in Montana, and another time when we went to Lake Powell in Arizona. There were a lot of birds and ducks in Montana, so I sat at the front of the board and watched them closely while Mom paddled to keep us moving along. On Lake Powell, it was such a lovely outing in the warm sunshine that I fell fast asleep, and Mom had to wake me up when we got back to shore. We went paddling again in Page, Arizona where we got to float through a slot canyon. Seeing those towering walls of striped rock on either side of us was pretty epic.

By the last several months of my life, mom had to pick me up to set me on the paddle board since I could no longer use my back right leg. Once I was situated in the middle of the board, I would lie down and let Mom squire me about the lake. It was so relaxing! I didn't even notice when my tail or back foot would trail along in the water as we paddled. I liked to lick the water off of my front paws and the paddle board but got annoyed when Mom would drip water on me from the paddle.

Catching food and paddle boarding weren't the only new tricks that I picked up in old age. When I stopped being able to use my back right leg due to the degenerative myelopathy, I learned to use my Walkin' Wheels® wheelchair to go for walks. I didn't love the process of being strapped in at first, but I got used to it and appreciated that it allowed me to still go on my regular walks. I already told you about how great walking is for your health, so I'll leave it at that.

Just like me, you can learn new things no matter your age. Using your body and mind in new ways can keep you healthy. Don't ever let anyone tell you that you're too old to do something you want to do. It's good for your mind to continue to learn as you age. Learning in later life is a way to protect the brain against aging because it promotes "neuroplasticity" (according to scientists, that's the brain's ability to develop new neural pathways).

You don't have to take my word for it, according to Michael Mosley in the BBC article *Learn Something New to Boost Your Brain*, "Not only does learning a new skill help your mental health, it can actually change the way your brain is wired – helping encourage the growth of new brain cells and new connections…new encouraging research is showing that our brain's plasticity is retained well into old age – far later than once thought."[1] Besides that, trying new things prevents you from getting too stuck in your ways.

Maintain a Healthy Respect for Water

"A healthy fear of the sea keeps you afloat."
—Unknown

From a young age, I enjoyed wading in the water. I would run around in ankle-deep water and enjoy every second, but I had zero interest in swimming despite Mom's attempts to get me to try. She would get into the freezing water at the end of a hike and try to coax me in, but I would always head straight to shore. I was content with wading.

One afternoon we were at a river after a hike and some rafters came by. I had never seen a raft before and got really excited. I thought it was so cool that they could be out in the middle of the river on a floatation device. I showed my excitement by running back and forth, watching them the whole time they were in sight.

Mom loved the water from the time she was a kid. She told me about days when she would spend hours in the pool in the backyard of her childhood home. She grew up in New Hampshire, where there were a lot of bodies of water nearby. There was a large pond and two lakes within a few miles of home, so she used to water ski as a kid and later got a kayak. When she moved out on her own, she lived near a river and a reservoir, and in summer she would kayak at least once a week. Mom always loved the ocean too, even though she lived at least an hour away from New Hampshire's bit of coastline. When she moved to Colorado, it was hard for her to be so far away from the ocean and there weren't many lakes and rivers nearby. But she found places to use her kayak, and later her stand-up paddle board, and most of her vacations involved visiting the ocean.

That's why she was so intent on bringing me to the ocean so that I could experience it myself. She drove in the car with Mala and me for three days each way to bring us to California. Dad wasn't a fan of road trips at the time and didn't have as much vacation time from work, so he flew in a plane to meet us. Mala and I were so excited to see him when we picked him up from the airport. I enjoyed running around on the beach, and chasing the water back out after a wave would break. But, when a new wave would start coming towards me, I would high tail it out of there. I didn't trust water that came after me! The ocean also tasted funny, so I definitely did not drink it! Even though we didn't love the ocean water as much as Mom, she was content that we at least loved the beach.

Lakes and reservoirs are mostly safe to enjoy from a paddle board, but always pay attention to the weather, to which way the wind is blowing, and if there's a current. Paddle against the current and wind on the way out, so that when you start to get tired and turn around, you'll be moving with it on the way back and won't have to paddle as hard.

We had a lot of great experiences on the water, but we also had one scary experience on a Stand Up Paddleboard (SUP) at Union Reservoir in Colorado. There weren't any storms in the forecast, so we headed out as a family. I was on Mom's board and Mala was on Dad's. When we were out in the middle of the lake, the wind picked up and it was fierce! It was so strong it blew all of us who were out on the lake to the far east side. The wind even picked up some boards and flung them against the rocks. Mom was lucky to have me (the survivalist) on her board because my weight helped keep our SUP anchored while we tried to direct the board as the wind pushed us across the lake. When we got close to shore, I somehow fell off the SUP. At first, I was scared, but then I realized that the water was shallow enough that I could stand, so I immediately regained my cool.

Mom and Dad pulled the boards, and Mala and me, to safety, and Dad hitched a ride back to our car and came to pick us all up. Mala was pretty scared, but I told her everything would be okay because at least it wasn't thundering! That experience wasn't the best, but it didn't deter me from wanting to do more paddle boarding.

I may not have been a swimmer, but I always enjoyed participating in water activities with Mom—safely! Bodies of water, like rivers, lakes, and the ocean, can be a lot of fun, but you also have to respect the power of water. Some rivers rush quickly and could pull you downstream if you're not careful, so it's best to stay where the water isn't too deep. The beach is a blast, but the ocean is vast and powerful, and the waves are no joke. When in doubt, stay on shore!

Life is Short, So Don't Put Off What You Want To Do

"You must live in the present, launch yourself on every wave, find your eternity in each moment. Fools stand on their island opportunities and look toward another land. There is no other land; there is no other life but this."
—Henry David Thoreau

Generally speaking, humans get to spend a lot more time on Earth than us dogs. Our life spans are usually fifteen years or less, while many humans live to be eighty years old. That said, there are no guarantees. You never know what tomorrow will bring, so you need to live your life now. Don't sit on the sidelines waiting for the perfect time. The time is now. You only get one chance, so you might as well spend your time on what you love.

I've told you about the things that made me happy, and how I focused my energy on joy, and having adventures. I lived a full life. I saw and did many things that a lot of people don't ever see and do. It's a shame to spend your life on the things that don't matter. If you expend all of your energy worrying about the little things, there will be no time left to enjoy the things that make life worth living.

Some people prioritize work in the hopes that when they retire, they can do all of the things that they put off their entire lives. But what if retirement never comes, or by the time you get there you're too ill or injured to adventure? Sure, I get that humans need to make money to have a home and food. However, money isn't everything. Life experiences are important too. If you spend all of your time working, you'll miss out on moments of joy with your friends and family. You'll get to the end and realize how much you missed by working late just to get a project done that probably wasn't that big of a deal anyway.

Before she left the corporate world to start her own business Mom used to work a lot of hours. During those years she went into the office all day, she would often bring her computer home to continue working after we had dinner and went for a walk. It wasn't until after her heart attack that she realized how much she had been sacrificing for her job. She started to take more vacations, including one that lasted for six weeks! I missed her when she was traveling around South and Central America during her sabbatical, but I also applauded her for adventuring and expanding her horizons. She created memories that she'll look back on in old age and be glad that she got to walk the Inca trail, see Machu Picchu, scuba dive with hammerhead sharks, and bike between wineries in Argentina and Chile. She'll always remember her time learning to teach yoga in Costa Rica, and the people she met there. I was proud of her for turning her priorities around, and therefore, her life! She started living. It was even better when I got to go along on adventures.

We did so many fun things in the time that we had together. I'm glad that Mom realized how precious life is, and valued spending time on the things that we loved. She traveled the world, and I would give her a big greeting when she returned. She usually brought something back for me because she felt bad that I couldn't join her for all of those adventures. When we could drive to a fun place, we'd go together. I was great in the car because I knew it meant that we were getting to do something fun.

Stop postponing your life. Start doing what you want to do. Make a list of the things you want to do, the places that you want to see, and the experiences you want to have. Then start doing them. Some might take more time and effort than others, but some might be easier to do. Start living the life you want, so that you don't end up looking back someday and realizing that you never really lived. That would be the greatest tragedy.

Be In Awe of the World around You

"In every walk with nature, one receives far more than he seeks."
—John Muir

The world is full of magic if you take the time to pay attention. Nature in particular contains unlimited examples of what a wonderful world we live in—from the pink of the sky at sunrise, to buds becoming flowers, and the sound of a hummingbird's wings.

The problem is that a lot of people barrel through their lives, spending too much time on their devices, and thinking that material things will make them happy, and they fail to notice all of the treasures that surround them.

Dogs are much better at awe. We experience the world through our senses, and we engage as many as we can when exploring something or somewhere new. Mom told me that science has shown that engaging more of your senses at any given moment will help you remember the details of it. Have you ever noticed that a certain scent can take you right back to your grandma's kitchen, or a song reminds you of your first dance with the boy you liked in middle school? Our senses make the world feel more alive, and the longer you pause to take it all in, the better you'll remember those precious moments that make life worth living. And, let me tell you, those moments are not going to be about your promotions or paychecks, but about the time you spent with loved ones, or experiencing a new place.

While I wasn't super happy about sleeping in a tent, there were other aspects of our camping and road trips that I appreciated—like watching the sunset over the lake, going for hikes in wild places, and experiencing the natural world in destinations like Lake Powell, the Grand Canyon, and Glacier National Park's Going-to-the-Sun road. Dogs weren't allowed on the trails at Glacier National Park, but I had my head out the window the whole time while we drove along the Going-to-the-Sun road. The jagged mountain peaks were even more impressive than the ones we have in Colorado.

I spent a lot of time looking out over the Grand Canyon on my last road trip. Mom promised me that it would be worth the drive for me to experience the ultimate vista, and she was right. It was amazing—all of the colors in the rocks, the river down below, and the ever-changing sky. I loved it, so I didn't mind how many times I had to be strapped into my Walkin' Wheels® wheelchair while we were there. We walked all along the rim trail, and I was sure to pause at each overlook. I needed a little help in some areas where the trail wasn't flat or had some obstacles, but it was worth the effort.

Take the time to pause and notice the world around you. If you pay attention, you'll start to see how amazing it is—the natural world in particular. Watch the sunrise or the sunset to see how the sun paints the sky. Stop to smell the wildflowers on your walk (as I mentioned previously, daily walks are good for your health). Enjoy the sound of the birds chirping, and the wind in the leaves. Run your hands through your dog's fur and enjoy how soft it is. Savor the taste of a morsel of your favorite food. There's so much to be grateful for, but it requires slowing down to take it all in.

Don't Simply Express Your Joy; Unleash It Wholeheartedly!

"I am grateful for what I am and have.
My life is full of simple pleasures."
—Henri Frederic Amiel

I was full of spunk for most of my life. I only started to relax a little bit when I was around nine or ten years old. I had a lot of energy, and I lived my life to the fullest. Even in my elder years, I still expressed my joy for the things that I loved—like hiking and pizza.

There was never any question of whether I was having a good time when we were out on a trail. My smile said it all. I loved being out and about, enjoying nature, sniffing the interesting scents, and greeting all of the people we came across on our adventures.

I didn't mind being in the car for long periods. I would just sleep in my bed in the back of the car and save my energy so I could enjoy myself when we got to our destination. I was always eager to get out of the car and had a hard time containing myself when we arrived somewhere for a walk, a hike, or even just a meal out on a patio. When I was young, I would rarely sit down when we ate out at a restaurant. I wanted to make sure Mom didn't forget to share some bites with me. When I got older, Mom and Dad would bring a blanket for me so that I could comfortably lay down next to the table.

Even though I didn't like silly games like fetch, I did like to play with my toys. I especially loved squeaky toys – the more squeakers the better. I particularly liked my stuffed lamb, which had four separate squeakers, so I could bite down anywhere and be rewarded with a squeak. I also loved my bear, which had squeakers in each of the four paws and one in the body. Mom and I both thought he should have had a squeaker in his nose, too.

I tended to bark a lot, but it was just another way that I expressed my joy and excitement. Sometimes it got me into trouble with the neighbors, but what was I supposed to do? I needed to share my thoughts, and barking was my way to do it.

I didn't hold back my excitement when my humans returned home from being away. It didn't matter how long they were gone, I made sure they always knew how much they had been missed. I thought I was wholehearted in expressing my joy, but my little sister Mala was even more so. She would zoom around the yard in big circles at top speed at least a few times whenever our parents got home. They called it her Indy 500. When we moved to the mountains, she didn't have a big enough flat area to satisfy her, so she would include the steep hill in her laps. Mala ran that route so often that she ended up wearing a path into the ground.

We dogs are not shy about expressing ourselves. I loved my life and I made sure everyone around me knew it. People can sometimes get bogged down in their responsibilities and all the expectations they pile upon themselves (or allow others to add). They forget how to have fun and express joy. We have the power to choose a life filled with joy. The more you can fill your life with the things that light you up and make you feel alive, the happier you'll be. Make those things a priority and carve out time in your day—every day—to do what brings you joy. When was the last time you let loose and unleashed your joy? If you had to think about it, it's been too long.

Don't Stop Learning

"The greatest danger for most of us is not that our aim is too high and we miss it, but that it is too low and we reach it."
—Michelangelo

E xploring the world is great for many reasons, one of which is that you can expand your horizons. I'm a firm believer in life-long learning. None of us can ever know everything there is to know, so it's important to continue to push yourself. Expand the boundaries of what you already understand so you can see how far you can go.

Learning new things keeps your mind sharp, and it makes life interesting. When you stop asking questions or don't want to challenge your ideas, assumptions, and existing knowledge, then you miss out on a lot. There's always something to learn. Things are always changing and evolving, and you have to keep learning so that you can evolve, too – otherwise, you get left behind. A lot of people get stuck in their ways of being and thinking and don't want anyone or anything to challenge them. That's no way to live, and, frankly, it can make you grumpy because everything around you will be moving on and leaving you behind with your outdated views.

I was always happy to learn new things. I told you about how I discovered paddle boarding when I was in my later years. I learned how to use my Walkin' Wheels® wheelchair when I lost the use of my back right leg. I also learned new tricks, like catching treats tossed my way. If I hadn't been willing to do those things, I would have missed out on a lot of good stuff. I expanded my world by being up for new things.

I was eight years old when my little sister, Mala, was introduced to the family. Before that, I didn't play with other dogs. I didn't mind running around and letting them chase me, but I didn't wrestle with them. When my little sister arrived in our home, my parents explained that I needed to teach her. I showed her how to walk on a leash, how to secure the backyard by chasing the squirrels up the trees, and how to get treats from Mom. Mala taught me some things, too. She liked to play, so I started playing tug of war and wrestling with her. It was different, but it was interesting to do new things since I trusted her not to hurt me. We both knew when things had gone too far, or one of us was no longer in the mood for roughhousing.

Mom was big on learning new things, too. I especially liked her experimentation with perfecting homemade pizza. She spent a lot of time making pizza and figuring out the best recipe and process for the perfect dough. We ate a lot of pizza during that time. Mom also started learning to speak Spanish. She never became an expert, but she enjoyed being able to order food and communicate when traveling in Spanish-speaking countries. Mom was always learning about different cultures and researching places to travel. She already had a master's degree when she went back to school to become a health coach. Mom took a lot of classes—whether it was yoga, language, writing, or cooking, she made a point to learn something new at least once a year.

I suppose that was just one more thing we had in common. Mom and I both saw the value in learning new things. We liked to challenge ourselves and got bored if we weren't expanding our horizons. Life is much more interesting when you are open to educating yourself. It's good to be a beginner again, to let go of what you think you already know. Having a beginner's mind opens so many more possibilities. When you're unwilling to grow and transform, your world is smaller and more confined. I'd rather be open and receptive to this big, wonderful world we live in.

Never Stop Exploring

"What we know is a drop, what we don't know is an ocean."
—Isaac Newton

I lived a life full of adventure. I told you a lot about them and how much I loved exploring new places. This great big world provides endless opportunities for new experiences. Some people, even when traveling, are closed to what is happening around them. They get caught up in what they already know and believe, and don't open their eyes or minds to other ways of being.

The way to really explore a place is to go in with no expectations and have your eyes wide open—and your nose, too. Discover your surroundings by seeing with fresh eyes. Engage your senses and take the time to get to know everything. You can even do this in places you've visited many times. Imagine you are experiencing it for the first time. Make it your intention to discover something new about it. Take your time and notice how the light shines through the trees, or how the time of year affects how things appear. When you see the world in this way, you will never stop exploring.

As I got older, I slowed down, which gave me even more opportunity to take things in. When Mom and Dad took me to the Grand Canyon, I stopped at each vista we came across along the Rim Trail and paused to look out. We walked at different times of day while we were there, so I took in the way the light changed the colors of the canyon. I stood at each lookout for a long time and appreciated the natural beauty and wonder. I was so happy to have the opportunity to experience such an amazing place. My parents were always making up road trip songs and they loved watching me look out at the vistas so much that the one they made up on that trip included the line, "Take it all in."

I explored the world right up until my final days. I wasn't able to hike anymore, but I could still go for walks with my Walkin' Wheels®, sniff along the trails, say hello to people and fellow dogs, and enjoy the sun on my fur. Mom still took me paddle boarding on the lake, so I could watch the birds and dip my feet in the water. Experiencing the world around you is what makes life worth living. We live in a grand world with so much to see and experience. All you need to do is open your eyes and your heart. So, get out of your bubble, take it all in, and never stop exploring.

It's Okay to Accept Help When You Need It, but Don't Be Helpless

---

"Our greatest glory in living lies not in never falling, but in rising every time we fall."
—Ralph Waldo Emerson

People are lucky because, unlike us dogs, you almost always have a choice, which means you don't have to be a victim of your circumstances. If you're unhappy with something you can change the situation. If you can't change it, you still have the option to accept wherever you are until you can.

I was independent and could mostly take care of myself. I did need Mom to feed me since she kept my food hidden away from me due to my habit of eating whatever was accessible. When I first started having trouble making the jump into the back of the car, I was frustrated. Mom bought me a ramp to walk up, but I didn't like it and refused to use it. When she would try to pick me up, I would jump at the same time to prove that I could do it without any help. But, after I missed reaching the bumper a couple of times and fell back, I realized it was time to start accepting a little bit of help. I'd still try to jump to give us both a little momentum, but I would let Mom lift me into the back of the car.

I believe that you should keep doing as much as you can for as long as possible, but, when you can no longer safely do what you need to do, that's when you should let the people who love you help you. There was no reason for me to use that Walkin' Wheels® device until I could no longer get my back right leg to move. Mom was trying to get me used to the wheels when I could still walk on my own, so I made it abundantly clear that I didn't need them yet. However, when the day came that I did need those wheels, I stood still while Mom strapped me into that odd contraption. It was weird not having my back feet on the ground, but I hadn't felt my feet in a while anyway. The wheels enabled me to still go for my walks, and that's what mattered. It turns out, that people thought it was pretty great that I was walking on the trails with my wheels. They would congratulate me and make a big deal about it, but I was just doing what I had to so I could stay active.

Mom brought me for acupuncture once a month from the time that I started showing signs of degenerative myelopathy. I didn't love going to the vet, but I knew they were all just trying to help me, so I lay calmly on the bed to receive my treatment. It helped that they gave me lots of treats. When things with my suspected disease progressed, I started going to physical therapy once a week. While I didn't like having to walk on the water treadmill (it was like a bath with exercise at the same time, and I never liked baths), I didn't mind the other parts of my sessions. All of those things (like the laser and standing on balance boards) did make me feel better and kept me mobile as long as possible. After my sessions, Mom would take me to get a "pup cup" from Starbucks or French fries from Wendy's on the way home. She figured by that time in my life, I could indulge a bit without too much fear of the sugar and fat content.

If you can do something on your own, then by all means, do it. It's good to develop confidence by challenging yourself and testing your limits. Mom enjoyed doing stuff like that. She even started doing triathlons in her thirties. She wasn't the least bit helpless.

Mom traveled alone once in a while so she could have experiences during which she could do whatever she wanted to do and not worry about anyone else. She felt good about being able to navigate on her own. She also did a lot of stuff around the house. When something would break, her first call was to her dad, but he was more than 2,000 miles away. He could give her some ideas but it was up to her to try them. She managed to fix plenty of things by herself. When the job was too big or complicated, she'd call someone else to come and help. I was proud of her for being so self-sufficient—it gave her confidence. She would always joke about wishing a neighborhood kid would offer to shovel the driveway or mow the lawn, but she kept right on doing those things herself. Mom was grateful to have someone share some of the burdens of keeping up a home when Dad moved in, but she still did her fair share of stuff around the house.

Remember, it's okay to ask for help, but doing things for yourself is a good way to stay sharp. Mom said that she'd gotten a little soft living in Colorado. Apparently, life had been harder when she lived in New Hampshire. I disagreed, I thought she was pretty badass being a single woman making it on her own. I loved that about her. Just one more thing we had in common—our ability to take care of ourselves.

Find Your Voice, and Communicate Openly

"It's better to speak your mind and tell the truth than to stay quiet and lie to yourself."
—Unknown

When Mom first adopted me from the shelter, I had kennel cough. I didn't make much noise because I wasn't feeling great. Once I recovered, I started using my voice and never stopped. I had all kinds of ways to communicate even though I couldn't speak the same way that humans can. I could bark, whine, growl, grumble, or yip. I liked barking the most. I could bark in many different pitches to communicate whether I was excited, upset, hungry, annoyed, or protective.

Mom said I had a deep voice for a medium-sized dog. When we were just a couple of single girls living alone, Mom liked that I sounded big and intimidating when I'd bark from the backyard. Both of us felt safer when I would bark if I felt an intruder was nearby. When I was a puppy, Mom was a bit worried that someone would try to steal me, so she put a lock on the fence. But I was pretty sure that if I was in the back yard my bark would scare away anyone who tried to come into our yard.

I wasn't afraid to tell others what I thought. I could use my bark to let other dogs know if I wanted them to stay away, or if I was willing to run around with them a bit. I could yip at Mom if it was getting close to dinner time, and she was still working on her computer and oblivious to the fact that it was time to eat. If she ignored me, I would employ my low-grade, almost imperceptible whine. While it wasn't nearly as loud as my bark, it was effective. That under-my-breath whine drove Mom crazy, so she would give in and feed me to get me to stop bugging her. As I got older, I started asking for dinner earlier and earlier to see just how soon I could get fed. Dad was easier to break than Mom.

Finding and using your voice is an important part of life. You need to be able to communicate what you need and let people know how you feel. I had a lot to say and wasn't afraid to use my voice. I mostly barked since that allowed me to express most of what I needed to share. I didn't grumble or growl much, but I did when it was necessary. If you don't let others know when you need space, they might not give it to you.

Mom wasn't a big fan of conflict, so sometimes she wouldn't speak up when someone was upsetting her. She'd try to brush it off and move on but eventually it would lead to bigger problems, and she'd have to tell the person how she felt. In my humble opinion, it's better to just say what you mean and how you feel in the moment and save everyone from guessing whether there's anything wrong. Open lines of communication make relating to others easier.

Mom sometimes worried she was imposing treatment on me when we started doing all the stuff to slow the progression of my degenerative myelopathy and help me walk—like the toe-ups, booties, acupuncture, physical therapy, and Walkin' Wheels® wheelchair. She talked to a friend who is skilled at communicating with animals. After Mom explained our relationship to this friend, the woman assured her that our lines of communication were open and functional. Of course, they were! I could have told her that. I always let her know if I wasn't in the mood for something. I didn't always love all that stuff, but I knew it was all intended to help me, and I was still happy to be able to go on walks and other adventures. I wasn't done living.

When I was ready to call it quits, I did let Mom know. She was so sad that night and the next morning when I was hurting and she couldn't fix it. The lady who came to the house to help me transition to the other side told Mom that I was easing the burden by letting her know I was ready so she didn't have to make that decision alone. We had our last words with each other on my bed in the living room. Mom cried a lot, but by then we had said everything that needed to be communicated. I felt her stroking my fur and kissing my snout as I slipped away from my body. I still communicate with her from the realm where I am now. I send her little reminders of our life together and my love for her. Be sure to tell those who you love how much you care while you can. They sure will appreciate hearing the words.

Do. Dream. Explore. It's Better To Do It First and Ask For Forgiveness Later.

"Plunge boldly into the thick of life, and seize it where you will, it is always interesting."
—Johann Wolfgang von Goethe

I mostly did whatever I wanted throughout my life, knowing that it's better to ask for forgiveness later rather than trying to get permission first. There will always be naysayers who think you can't do whatever it is you want to do, but don't listen to them. Maybe they're just jealous because you're doing something they wish they could have done, but never took the chance. Or maybe they underestimate your abilities, but no one ever really knows what they're capable of doing until they try.

You might try and fail, but it's better than never trying at all. I once chased after a chipmunk in the yard and ended up falling off of the retaining wall into the parking area. Mom was worried for a second, but I popped right up and showed her I was fine.

You might do something and get in trouble for not conforming to what others think you should do, but I promise it will still have been worth it. I did all kinds of things I wasn't supposed to do. Mom sometimes got mad at me for my escapades, but I would give her my best grin and, sure enough, she would forgive me. Sometimes it would take a bit longer if I did something she *really* disliked, but she always got over it.

Mom used to get hung up on what others expected her to do and be, but after surviving her heart attack, she got a bit better at listening to her own heart and gut. She started spending more time on the things that made her happy. When she wanted to leave her job in Denver for a more flexible position that allowed her to work at home, her manager told her she shouldn't leave. I'm glad she did it anyway because it was nice to have her at home more often. We could have lunch together and go for afternoon walks while it was still nice outside. When she decided to focus solely on her own business, she was nervous about giving up a steady paycheck, but it was nice to see her spending time doing the things that brought her joy.

There's a lot of pressure on people to do what is considered "normal," but it's okay to break the mold. I encourage it! Society puts a lot of labels and expectations on women in particular. Some people judge women like my Mom who decide not to have human kids. Mom's life was full with her four-legged kids and the business she built. It might be hard for some to understand, but it's what makes her happy and that's all that matters.

Dream big and commit your life to doing what you want. You only get one chance, so you might as well spend your life on what makes you feel most like you, even if it means disappointing some people. For the most part, the people who love you will love you no matter what, and the people who judge you aren't worth your time. So, go ahead and do, dream, and explore. As Paulo Coelho wrote in *The Alchemist*, "Wherever your heart is, that is where you'll find your treasure."[1] If you don't follow your dreams, you may never find them, and wouldn't that be a shame?

Dogs Know Best, and Humans Need Us

Dogs do speak, but only to those who know how to listen.
—attributed to Orhan Pamuk

I had a lot to say my whole life. Mom and Dad used to joke that if I could talk, they'd be in trouble. But the truth is that I spoke to them all the time, just in my own language. They didn't always pick up what I was trying to say … but a lot of the time, they did. Mom especially knew what my different tones and expressions meant. I had a lot of ways to express my thoughts and feelings. I could bark, whine, look at them a certain way with my expressive eyes, move my ears forward or back, wag my tail (or tuck it if the situation called for that), nudge their hand … there are a lot of ways that a dog can communicate with people. Not all people know how to listen, though. Some people underestimate how smart we are.

I hope that from what I've shared with you in this book, you've gained an understanding of all the ways dogs know best. People have been living in harmony with dogs for a long time, so it seems you do get that you need us. We can be a loving companion, a protector, a friend, a loyal sidekick, and a fellow adventurer. We can ease your stress and anxiety, we can lick your tears when you're sad, or share in your joy when you're happy. We are part of the family. We add another dimension to your life. We help you live longer, happier lives just by living with you. I know Mom would have still done a lot of fun things even if she hadn't had me by her side, but we both know everything was better because we got to do it together.

I know she needed me, and the truth is I needed her, too. We were soulmates, and both were fortunate that the universe brought us together on that fateful day in June of 2006. Mom told me the story of the day we met many times. It's no coincidence that the puppy she was on her way to meet got adopted by someone else—he or she wasn't meant for her. I was.

As much as she tried to train me to be a good dog, *I* was the one who taught *her*. I helped her to see what the important things in life are and to let go of the things that weren't part of her path. Mom grew in the years that we were together. She made mistakes, but I was there to stand by her side and help her take the lesson and leave the pain. Mom appreciated me and accepted my quirks because she knew it didn't matter if I walked calmly on a leash or never barked. I might not have been what people call a "good" dog, but I was a smart dog. I knew how to live and how to love. I did both with enthusiasm.

I lived a full life. I did what I was put on this Earth to do, which was to take care of Mom in the best way I could, the way only I could. As I watch over her, I see that I did a great job. She took my lessons to heart, and I'm proud of all she's accomplished. She's a kind, loving, courageous, adventurous person who has dedicated her life to helping others. Mom figured out her purpose in this life, and she's doing it well.

Mom still has the siblings I groomed (not that you can do much to teach cats how to behave, but they're mostly okay), Mala, Mateo, and Kali. Dad loves and cares for her, which I knew he would. I still watch over my family and am glad they adopted another dog, Tessie, about a year after we said goodbye. My sister Mala has plenty of love to give, but I could tell a new puppy was an important piece of healing Mom's heart after she lost me.

I sent Tessie to Mom to fill the hole in her heart that appeared when I had to go. Like me, Tessie is a dog with a mind of her own and a spunky attitude, but she has a big heart. It turns out Mom needs a bit more cuddling these days, so Tessie does that for her. I can see that being with

CARRIE LEHTONEN

Tessie is helping Mom to heal, but we both know there will always be a special place in her heart for me.

My closing wish for you is that you, too, find that special dog who was meant for you. That you can communicate with him or her and are open to learning all they have to teach you. Open your heart to a dog, and you'll never be alone. Of course, it will hurt when your dog has to go, but it will have been worth it. I promise.

Epilogue

"Dogs come into our lives to teach us about love. They depart to teach us about loss. A new dog never replaces an old dog, it merely expands the heart."
—attributed to Erica Jong

This story has been told from Ella's point of view, but now it's my turn. I'm the one you've come to know as "Mom." I was the one who adopted Ella from the shelter in Denver, Colorado, and spent over fifteen wonderful years with her. I never thought of myself as her "owner." The reason she had the nickname of Queen is because I knew she was special. I didn't always listen at first, or understand right away, but I knew she was wise. Even as a puppy, she had an air about her – a look of someone beyond her years.

As cliché as it sounds, Ella's eyes were truly the windows to her soul. When I looked into those deep brown, almond-shaped eyes, I knew she was the one who was in charge. She had me wrapped around her paw, so to speak. She could get away with anything, and she knew it. I got mad at her now and then but never stayed that way for long.

In some ways Ella was predictable, but she was also full of surprises. I had to keep an eye on her in case, for example, she decided that the best course of action when teetering on a half-open car window would be to jump out into the road (that only had to happen once for me to never put the window too far down again).

In August 2021, Ella had grown weary of her battle with degenerative myelopathy (DM), and at fifteen years and eight months of age her soul was ready to leave her ailing body. We said goodbye as John, Mala, and I sat by her side on her bed in the living room—the only time she didn't give me the look that said, "Why are you on my bed?" The day Ella left her Earthly body was one of the hardest of my life. I was saying goodbye to my best friend, my companion. The following are the words I read to her that morning. I wasn't sure I would ever share these with anyone but her, but it seems only right to include them here after you've had all of these pages to get to know her.

Dear Ella,

It was fate that brought us together and love that fueled us over the past fifteen years. You are my best friend, and I'll forever cherish all of the memories we've made together – the good times and the not-so-good. From the day I met you, I knew you were special, and you've continued to show me how you are unlike any other dog I've ever met. From giving me that "what, do you think that I'm stupid?" look when I tried to get you to play fetch; your impeccable record of security detail in the backyard; claiming my recliner in the living room as your own since it was by the front window and allowed you to watch what was going on; deciding to take yourself for a walk around the pond when you got away from me (or exploring neighbors' garages – I mean, they were open, so clearly that was an invitation); your love of kids (who often have sticky fingers and are easy to take food from); the way you would hold onto my arm and shake when I'd come back from a trip; your "smile" when I'd get home from work that usually meant you did something naughty if you were smiling from the lower level of the house rather than coming all the way to the door to greet me; you proving that you're never too old to learn something new (from suddenly catching food thrown to you instead of letting it hit you in the face to starting to paddle board at nine years old). We never had a shortage of adventure, and even though you would ping-pong back and forth on our runs, you were always my favorite running partner. I'll always think of you on every hike, and how much you loved vistas (especially the one on Sanitas that I named after you).

You were a party animal who didn't want to go to bed while there were still people at the house—until you weren't, which didn't happen until you were over eight years old. Even though you would roll in cow manure, you avoided walking through mud if possible. You surprised us all that day when on a walk you suddenly jumped sideways into a pond that was completely green from all of the pollen. We still laugh about that incident to this day and wonder what the heck you were thinking as it was so uncharacteristic. You were full of surprises.

Remember that time I ended up with a criminal record because you enjoyed barking to tell the neighborhood that you were hungry when I wasn't home at 5:00 p.m. to feed you dinner some evenings? Always hungry, since you grew up on the streets—my little gluten-lover. Pizza will always trigger your "crazy," not to mention bread and dry pasta. I forgive you for all those days you got into the trash or stole food from a table or plate – you simply couldn't help yourself. If there's food, you eat it until it's gone—even if your belly hurts. You even got completely into the raised bed in the backyard to eat my veggies – corn, beans, and tomatoes, straight from the plants.

No one should have ever underestimated your determination and skill. Of course, you were going to unzip that backpack and eat a full bag of chocolate-covered raisins – who cares if people say dogs shouldn't eat raisins? Maybe you were just testing John to determine if he was worthy to enter our partnership. You certainly were clear about your opinion of the men in my life and helped me see the light when I was in a bad situation. Thank you for always guiding me (yeah, yeah, I know, the leash was for me, not you). You have the best survival skills: if you're in a blizzard, you dig a hole in the snow to wait it out; if there's a storm, you get in the tub; and if there's food, you eat it. When it was hot in the summer, you'd run from shady spot to shady spot on hikes.

Your kind heart extended to most people, and the cats that were part of the family (but definitely not those other cats, especially the ones that were mean to your cats), some dogs, and you even took Mala under your wing even though you made it perfectly clear that you didn't want a puppy (and she annoyed you constantly). Of course, all beds in the house belonged to you – even the tiny one that was supposed to be for the cats. You would growl and jump down from my bed when I would get in at night but would always come back up in the morning to let me know it was time for your breakfast. Forget about getting you to go outside first—food always comes before anything else. And, while I know you'll never forgive Kali for hissing at you when she was a two-pound kitten (which made you hide under the bed), you'll always be her best friend. All of us cherished you.

I'm sorry for making you go camping all of those times when we should have been sleeping in either our house or at a five-star hotel that catered to your needs. You loved your "wardrobe," and appreciated getting new collars from Uncle Keith. You'd sit up proud while I slipped a new collar over your head.

You were the best travel buddy, and we loved our road trips, even if Mala and John did not. I'm so glad I was able to take you to see the ocean, to Montana to see the vistas on Going-to-the-Sun Road—and to the ultimate vista at the Grand Canyon—and paddle boarding in Antelope Canyon. You were a trooper right up through this—the end. You didn't like accepting help, but you got great at walking on the water treadmill and walking in your wheels when that back leg would no longer function.

Ella, you are my best friend, my heart, and you will forever be with me. Anabelle will be there to greet you in heaven, and you'll get to meet all of my pets who came before you. I love you now and always.

Love,

Mom

P.S. Thank you for being the ring bearer at our wedding. I'm sorry you didn't get to come to the reception.

I will forever cherish the unconditional love Ella gave me and I will never forget her spunk and determination. While this letter doesn't even come close to expressing how much Ella meant to me, the lessons in this book provide a glimpse into the ways she touched my life and made me a better person for having been lucky enough for fate to bring us together. As a wise (unknown) person once said, "Some souls just resonate with yours on a different frequency. When you meet them, you understand why." That sums up my relationship with Ella. I can't quite explain it, but we were soulmates.

Notes

Your Person is Out There, So Don't Settle for Less

1. Larry Roemer, director. *Rudolph the Red-Nosed Reindeer*. 1964; Classic Media LLC, 2014.

Shake It Off

1. Taylor Swift. 2014. "*Shake it Off*." Track 6 on 1989. Big Machine Records, compact disc.

Hydrate

1. "*Water: How much should you drink every day?*" Mayo Clinic, last modified October 12, 2022, https://www.mayoclinic.org/healthy-lifestyle/nutrition-and-healthy-eating/in-depth/water/art-20044256.

Live in the Present Moment. And Be Curious About the World Around You.

1. Gene Baur, *Farm Sanctuary: Changing Hearts and Minds About Animals and Food* (New York: Touchstone A Division of Simon & Schuster, 2008), 225-26.

Life is an Adventure ... Climb Aboard!

1. Hunter S. Thompson, *The Proud Highway: Saga of a Desperate Southern Gentleman 1955-1967* (New

York: Ballantine Books: an imprint of The Random House Publishing Group, 1997), 1.

Live Your Passion: Never Stop Doing What You Love

1. Brendan Burchard, *The Motivation Manifesto: 9 Declarations to Claim Your Personal Power* (California: Hay House, Inc., 2014), 157.

You're Never Too Old to Learn New Tricks

1. Michael Mosley, "*Learn Something New To Boost Your Brain.*" *BBC,* April 25, 2021, https://www.bbc.co.uk/programmes/articles/20 hzn5LR2xLPhjVqXyD2Q2C/learn-something-new-to-boost-your-brain.

Do. Dream. Explore. It's Better To Do It First and Ask For Forgiveness Later.

1. Paulo Coelho, *The Alchemist* (San Francisco: HarperOne, 2014), 132.

Resources

Baur, Gene. *Farm Sanctuary: Changing Hearts and Minds About Animals and Food.* New York: Touchstone A Division of Simon & Schuster, 2008.

Burchard, Brendan. *The Motivation Manifesto: 9 Declarations to Claim Your Personal Power.* California: Hay House, Inc., 2014.

Coelho, Paulo. *The Alchemist.* San Francisco: HarperOne, 2014.

Mayo Clinic. *"Water: How much should you drink every day?"* Last modified October 12, 2022. https://www.mayoclinic.org/healthy-lifestyle/nutrition-and-healthy-eating/in-depth/water/art-20044256.

Mosley, Michael. *"Learn Something New To Boost Your Brain."* *BBC,* April 25, 2021, https://www.bbc.co.uk/programmes/articles/20hzn5LR2xLPhjVqXyD2Q2C/learn-something-new-to-boost-your-brain.

Roemer, Larry, director. *Rudolph the Red-Nosed Reindeer.* 1964; Classic Media LLC, 2014.

Swift, Taylor. 2014. "*Shake it Off.*" Track 6 on 1989. Big Machine Records, compact disc.

Thompson, Hunter S. *The Proud Highway: Saga of a Desperate Southern Gentleman 1955-1967*. New York: Ballantine Books: an imprint of The Random House Publishing Group, 1997.

Acknowledgments

When I started writing down the lessons I learned from Ella, I hadn't even thought about turning her stories into a book. Thanks to the team of editors and mentors from Elephant Academy's Find Your Voice course who gave me feedback on the article I wrote for Elephant Journal, *"Unleash your Joy" – & 9 Other Lessons from a Shelter Dog Who Became Queen.* The success of that article and the comments from readers made me realize the lessons could benefit others and that I should turn that one article into a manuscript of 40 lessons! Thanks to Waylon Lewis for creating Elephant Journal, the first place I ever publicly shared my writing other than my own website, and who created the course that gave me the confidence to publish a book.

I'm grateful to poet and comic John Roedel who led the writing workshop, the Unafraid Storyteller, I attended at the Art of Living Retreat Center in North Carolina where I first started calling myself a writer. Mr. Roedel gently encouraged me to share my story and kickstarted the process of sitting down to write my manuscript.

Thanks to my family and friends who always have my back and are ready with encouragement when I find myself weighed down with self-doubt. My love of animals started from birth. I grew up with dogs and cats, as well as fish, rabbits, and guinea pigs. My parents, Carl and Debra Lehtonen, instilled in me a love for animals and the belief that I can accomplish anything I set my mind to. My mom in particular always had a soft spot for animals, and our pets were part of the family. When I moved away for college and then work, my parents took care of the dogs who I couldn't bring with me. My brother, Keith Kolapakka, kept Ella stylish and in season by providing her with custom collars throughout her life from his business, CritterGear. Ella adored her uncle and appreciated it when he came to visit us in Colorado. I'm grateful to my in-laws, Jay and Bunnie Busch, who welcomed Ella and me into the family with open arms and wholeheartedly support my business and creative endeavors.

I wouldn't be here to write this book if it wasn't for my friends Mike Price and Keith Guastella who convinced me to go to the hospital the day I had a heart attack in 2009. Not only did they take me to the hospital, but sat there with me for hours while I waited to see a doctor and then while the cardiologist placed a stent in my coronary artery. They are my guardian angels. Thanks also to Edgar Luna who took care of Ella while I was in intensive care for three days, and brought her to see me when I was finally moved to a regular hospital room that allowed dogs. Seeing her lifted my spirits.

My former manager, Mike Kane, was the one who allowed me to leave work in the middle of the day to go to the shelter where I met and adopted Ella. He was also the one fostering the kittens whom I adopted eight years later. He was one of the most easygoing people I have ever known, and the only reason I was able to sustain working in a corporate environment for the years that I did. I worked for him twice, when I first moved to Colorado and again after my heart attack when he hired me back for a role that would allow me to work at home and have less stress. He was also the person who supported me in taking a sabbatical (which was not a common occurrence at the company we worked for) so that I could travel and continue my yoga teacher education, and who worked it out so that I could move to a part-time position while I was growing my own business. Mike passed away, but I'll always remember him fondly as the best manager I ever had and the one who helped me grow my four-legged family.

Thank you to all the staff and volunteers at the Denver Dumb Friends League where I adopted Ella. You provide a second chance for so many animals who have been abandoned, and who otherwise wouldn't stand a chance. I appreciate all of the organizations that rescue animals and find them loving homes, including New Hope Cattle Dogs Rescue of Colorado where we later adopted our puppy, Tessie.

Thanks to all of those who were part of Ella's life and treated her as the Queen she was. Thank you to Ella's many pet sitters over the years, and Cottonwood Kennels who understood that Ella preferred solo walks around the farm to being in the play area with other dogs. I always felt comfortable leaving her in your care.

Even though Ella didn't like going to the vet (what dog does?), she didn't mind seeing Lisa Fredericks, DVM at Broomfield Veterinary Hospital, who was generous with the treats. Dr. Fredericks was also the veterinarian who treated Anabelle's kidney disease and helped her to the other side when it was time. Thanks to the vet who treated Ella at the emergency animal hospital when she got into the chocolate-covered raisins.

I'm grateful to the team of people who helped Ella maintain her quality of life when she started showing symptoms of degenerative myelopathy. Dr. Shelley Brown at Harmony Veterinary Center was the veterinarian who provided acupuncture to keep Ella active as long as possible. The staff at Canine Rehabilitation & Conditioning in Englewood were always happy to see Ella even though she didn't always comply with what they wanted her to do. I appreciate Mark C. Robinson who started the company Walkin' Pets, which makes Walkin' Wheels®, the device that kept Ella active after she lost control over her back right leg. I'll never forget the compassion we were shown by Dr. Danielle of Lap of

Love who came to our house that morning in August of 2021 to help ease Ella's transition to the other side. She treated Ella with the utmost care and respect, tucking her in with a blanket on the stretcher to bring Ella to the car, and slowly driving away.

A special shout out to the numerous people who consoled me and provided advice and support when I was agonizing over the decision to schedule Ella to be euthanized, including my family, my dear friend Stephanie Boyd (who understands the pain of making that kind of decision), and Deb Matlock (Founder and Director of Wild Rhythms). Ultimately, Ella decided that she was ready to depart about a week and a half earlier than planned, relieving me of the burden of deciding when it was time. She took care of me right up until the end.

With this being my first book, I had a lot to learn about the entire process. I appreciate the time, care, and energy that my editor, Susan Crossman, put into this book. I was nervous about sending my manuscript to a professional because I had no idea if it was good enough, but she was reassuring and encouraging that Ella's story needed to be told. I appreciate the time that the cover designer, Alexander von Ness, put into working with me to create the perfect tribute to my girl. Many others took the time to speak with me about the process of publishing so that I could confidently independently publish this book.

I'm grateful to all of those who made contributions to help fund the design and printing of the book, including Joe Nitsche, Mike Vail, Keith Jones, Aarav and Anu Rao, Scott Busch, and Jay and Bunnie Busch.

Finally, a big thank you to my husband, John Busch, without whom I would not be able to spend my days doing what I love. He provides not only health insurance but loads of love and support for my work. John is my biggest cheerleader who always reminds me that I have what it takes when I get mired in self-doubt. He accepted Ella as she was, and helped me care for her, especially when she couldn't walk on her own. Only five months into dating me, he spent his New Year's Eve in the animal hospital with Ella after she ate a whole bag of chocolate-covered raisins. He loved her as much as I did. I wouldn't have been able to do it without him. John, who didn't grow up with pets, happily accepted the role of Dad to my four-legged kiddos. Even though he wasn't sure when I was set on adopting Mala, and later Tessie, he recognized how certain I was that they were the perfect dogs to join our family and agreed that we should adopt them. Ella and I both agree that you are my human soul mate. Thank you for being my best friend and partner in life.

About the Author

Carrie Lehtonen grew up in a small town in New Hampshire. She earned a Master's degree in Organizational Leadership and spent over 18 years working in Human Resources. After surviving a heart attack at 31 years old, Carrie chose to pursue an education in health and wellness. Carrie attended the Institute for Integrative Nutrition to become a Holistic Health Practitioner. She also trained to become a Registered Yoga Teacher and Educator.

Carrie eventually left her career in Human Resources to create Firefly Community LLC. She is committed to reducing the impact of heart disease and loves seeing people light up when they learn something new, challenge themselves beyond what they think they are capable of, and tap into their purpose.

Carrie is a life-long learner and loves to travel to experience different cultures and diverse natural environments. She lives in Evergreen, Colorado with her husband, two dogs, and two cats, where she enjoys hiking, mountain biking, trail running, paddle boarding, and writing. Her work has been featured in Elephant Journal, YOGA+ Life®, and Well magazine. For more on Carrie, visit fireflycommunity.com.

www.ingramcontent.com/pod-product-compliance
Lightning Source LLC
Chambersburg PA
CBHW020252130626
46549CB00005B/2182